BUSINESS DESKTOP PUBLISHING APPLICATIONS

JOB-BASED TASKS

Victoria Lyons
Technology Coordinator
Cooperative Educational Services Agency
Chippewa Falls, Wisconsin

Cynthia Ziegler
Computer Coordinator and Business Education
Cochran–Fountain City High School
Fountain City, Wisconsin

Developmental Editor	Russ Blixt
Copy Editor	Laura Beaudoin
Text Design	Mori Studio
Cover Design	Joan Silver
Desktop Production	Kathleen Oftedahl, Tim Heitman

ACKNOWLEDGEMENTS

We wish to thank the following instructors and technical experts who contributed to this workbook:

Tommy Carter
Sandra Chase
E. Jean Jillson

Roberta Moore
Steven Springer
Jean Travis-Odefey

Library of Congress Cataloging-in-Publication Data

Lyons, Victoria R.
    Business desktop publishing applications: job-based tasks /
Victoria Lyons, Cynthia Ziegler
      p. cm.
    ISBN 1-56118-398-9
    1. Desktop publishing. 2. Business writing—Automation.
I. Ziegler, Cynthia. II. Title.
Z286.D47L96 1994
686.2'2544—dc20   92-29533
                                                                               CIP

Text + 3.5" PageMaker DOS disks: ISBN 1-56118-398-9
Order Number: 41118
Text + 3.5" PageMaker MAC disks: ISBN 1-56118-400-4
Order Number: 05118

© 1994 by Paradigm Publishing Inc.
        Published by **EMC**Paradigm
        875 Montreal Way
        St. Paul, MN 55102
        (800) 535-6865
        E-mail publish@emcp.com

All rights reserved. No part of this publication may be reproduced, stored in a retrieval system, or transmitted in any form or by any means, electronic, mechanical, photocopying, recording, or otherwise, without the prior written permission of Paradigm Publishing Inc.

Printed in the United States of America.

10 9 8 7 6 5 4 3

Contents

Introduction 1
Unit 1   Applying Desktop Publishing Basics **3**
    Application   1   Creating a Presentation Document 5
    Application   2   Modifying the Presentation Document 9
    Application   3   Preparing a Resume 11
    Application   4   Creating an Agenda 15
    Application   5   Creating a Newsletter 19
               Unit 1   Performance Challenge 23
Unit 2   Enhancing Text and Page Layout **25**
    Application   6   An Overhead Transparency 27
    Application   7   Company Directory 31
    Application   8   Product Specification Sheet 35
    Application   9   Seminar Advertisement 39
    Application 10   Public Relations Sheet 43
    Application 11   Poster 47
    Application 12   Recruitment Advertisement 51
    Application 13   Survey 55
    Application 14   Advertising Flyer—Trifold Inside 59
    Application 15   Price List 63
               Unit 2   Performance Challenge 67
Unit 3   Enhancing Publications **69**
    Application 16   Company Directory with Logo 71
    Application 17   Product Specification Sheet with
                           Graphics 75
    Application 18   Enhanced Seminar Advertisement ... 79
    Application 19   Public Relations Sheet with
                           Illustration 81
    Application 20   Poster with Boxes and Rules 85
    Application 21   Recruitment Advertisement with
                           Graphics 87
    Application 22   Survey with Highlighting 89
    Application 23   Enhanced Trifold Advertising Flyer . 93
    Application 24   Price List with Illustrations 97
    Application 25   Floral Flyer 101

Application 26	Newsletter I	105
Application 27	Newsletter II	109
Application 28	Brochure I	113
Application 29	One-Page Resume	117
Application 30	Brochure II	119
Application 31	Organizational Chart	123
Unit 3	Performance Challenge	125

Unit 4   Designing Multipage Documents 129

Application 32	Newsletter I – Next Issue	131
Application 33	Newsletter II – Next Issue	135
Unit 4	Performance Challenge	137

Glossary 149

Introduction

This workbook contains exercises that challenge your ability to use your desktop publishing software. By working through these exercises, you will gain skill and confidence in using your software.

This workbook can be used along with the software manual as a reference and/or with teacher instruction. Each application contains step-by-step instructions, a rough layout called a plan including a miniature of a final document, and review questions.

Unit 1 is a quick overview of the basic capabilities of desktop publishing software. You will combine the elements of text and graphics to produce documents that are both attractive and functional.

Unit 2 delves into modifications that can be made to text and layout to enhance the readability of a document. You will create publications such as brochures, advertisements, flyers, and newsletters.

Unit 3 explores how graphics enhance the visual appeal of a document.

Unit 4 enables you to use your skills to produce multiple-page documents that employ several advanced desktop publishing capabilities.

Throughout this workbook you will read hints for producing documents that follow basic rules of good design. These hints will help you to develop an eye for what a well-laid-out document looks like. The applications in this workbook also introduce you to basic concepts and vocabulary of layout, typography, and graphics.

Several applications require the use of files completed in previous applications. Each individual unit introduction will point out the applications which require previously created files. These files can be retrieved from your data disk or from your instructor (in the event you did not complete the previous application.)

Unit 1
Applying Desktop Publishing Basics

The applications in this unit provide a review of basic desktop publishing capabilities. You will create, save, retrieve, and print publications. Applications also require you to import, delete, and modify text. Creating documents with multi-column layout requires learning how to import graphics.

Your finished documents will include an overhead transparency, resume, agenda, newsletter template, and a one-page newsletter. The Unit 1 Performance Challenge reviews the objectives presented in Application 1 through Application 5.

The file created in Application 1, DTP1, is necessary to complete Application 2. The template created in Application 5 is necessary to complete the Unit 1 Performance Challenge.

Name _____
Section _____ Date _____

Application 1 Creating a Presentation Document

Your firm has been hired to create an overhead transparency for a manufacturing firm. The transparency should show monthly growth of sales compared to forecasted growth since the beginning of the year. The transparency master will include a bar chart and an appropriate title. The graphic file has been created for you. You now are ready to create a new file to incorporate these elements.

1. Create a new one-page file in portrait (tall, or vertical) layout. Use the default margin settings.

> **Hint** Do not crowd the page with text and/or graphics. The blank space on a page is referred to as white space. White space in a document gives the reader's eyes a chance to rest and helps the reader to focus on the message. The amount of white space varies with the purpose of the message.

2. Decide where to place the table so it is centered vertically. Check plan 1 for correct placement.
3. Create the heading "SALES VS. FORECAST."
4. Import the graphic CHARTA. Place it below the heading. Depending on your software, you may need to adjust the size of the graphic.
5. Arrange both title and chart so they are centered on the page.
6. Save the presentation document as DTP1.
7. Proof your work. Make any corrections or adjustments. Save again if necessary.
8. Print the document.

9. Proof the printed document. Make any corrections or adjustments. Print again if necessary. Save again if necessary.
10. Close the file.

> Complete the entire exercise before answering the review questions.

Review

1. What is the purpose of this presentation document?

2. Who is the audience?

3. Is the layout appropriate for the audience and purpose?

4. Is your document centered vertically and horizontally?

5. What is the procedure for importing a graphic?

6. What is the procedure for sizing the graphic?

7. In your opinion, what is missing from the document?

8. What is the procedure to move a graphic?

9. What are the default margins set in your desktop publishing software?

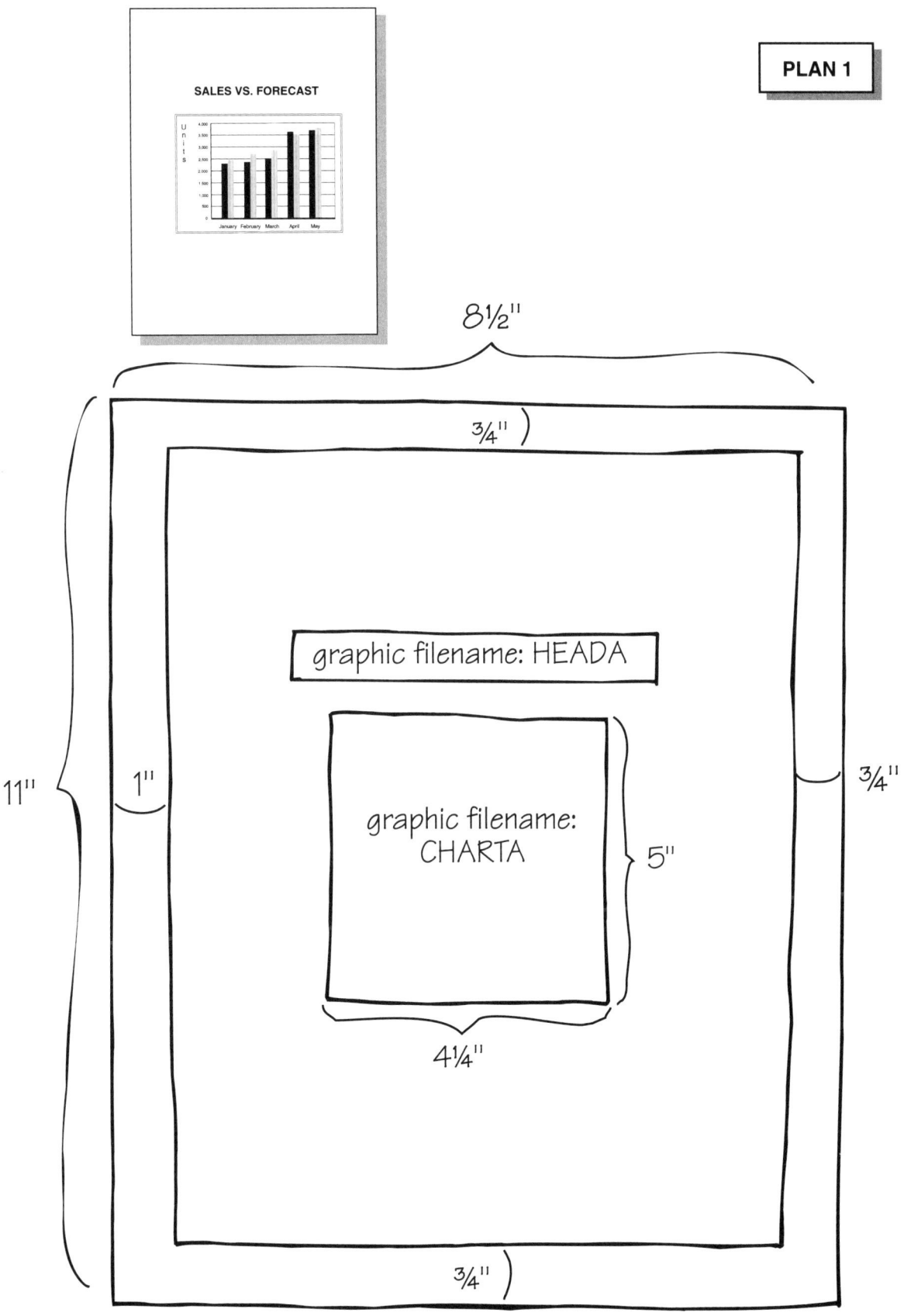

*Note: Margins may vary as they are the default settings.

Creating a Presentation Document • 7

Name _____
Section _____ Date _____

Application 2 Modifying the Presentation Document

The legends were missing from the overhead transparency master you created in application 1. You will modify the transparency you created in application 1 by adding a graphic and text.

1. Open DTP1.
2. Import the graphic LEGEND and superimpose in the upper left-hand corner of the chart, if possible, or below the chart on the right side. You may need to adjust the size and position of this graphic. Refer to plan 2.

Hint Placement of legend information is very important in business graphics. The legend must clearly identify the parts of the chart and be placed in an easy-to-read area.

3. Save the document as DTP2.
4. Proof your work. Make any corrections or adjustments. Save again if necessary.
5. Print the document.
6. Proof the printed document. Make any corrections or adjustments. Print again if necessary. Save again if necessary.
7. Close the file.

Complete the entire exercise before answering the review questions.

Review

1. Is there a sufficient amount of white space to allow the viewer to focus on the message of the transparency?

   _____
   _____

2. What design factors must you consider when working with business graphics?

   _____
   _____

9

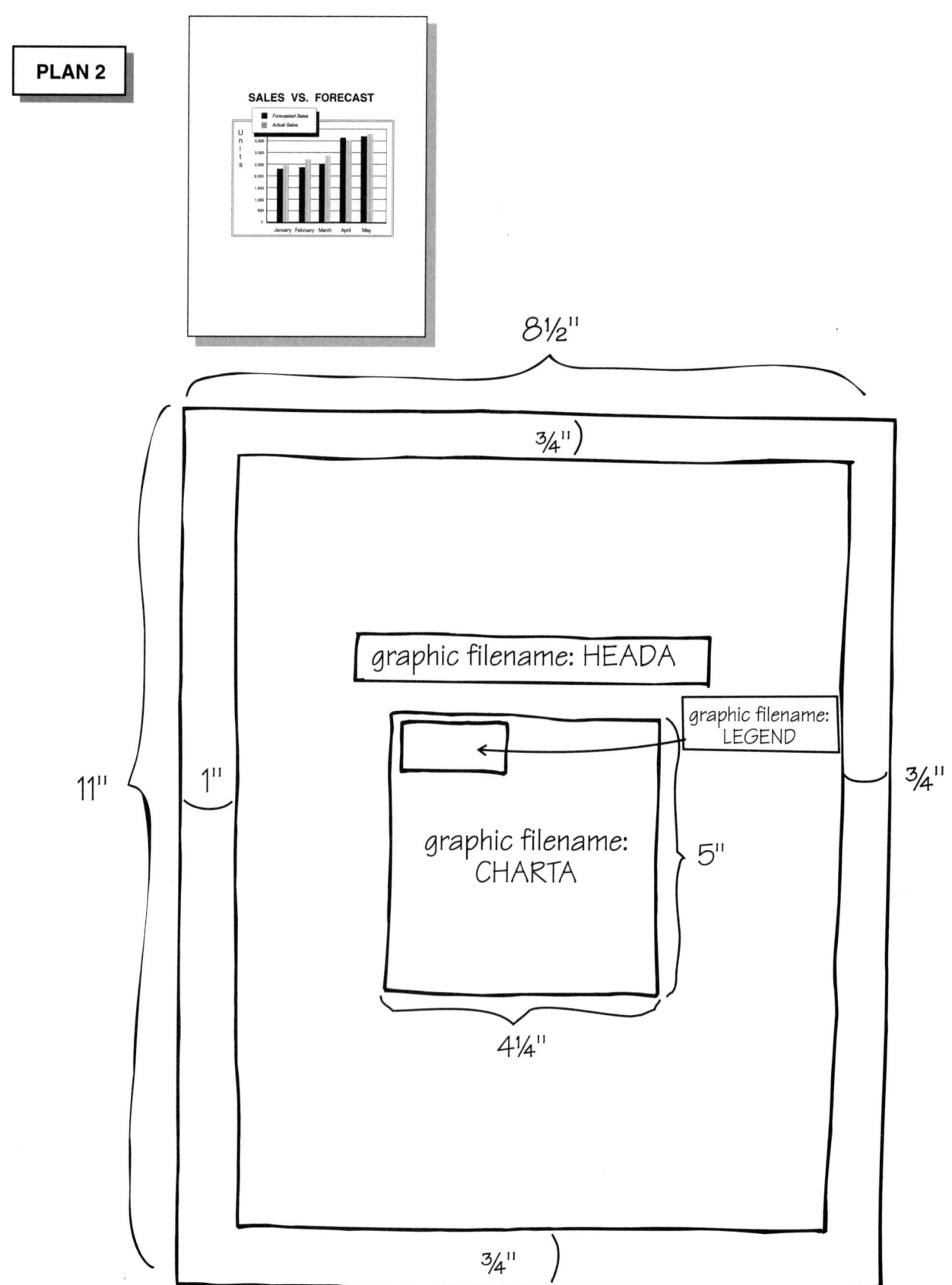

Name _____
Section _____ Date _____

Application 3 Preparing a Resume

In this application, you prepare a resume for a client. You must lay out the page. The client already has a resume keyed; however, through desktop publishing you are able to enhance the resume to give it a professional appearance. Resumes should be both eye-catching and easy to read. Generally, resumes should be simple in design.

1. Create a new one-page file in portrait (tall, or vertical) layout. Refer to plan 3.
2. Use the default margin settings.
3. Import the text RESUME3 and place immediately below the top margin in the left-hand corner. Center the text of the heading. Enlarge the type size of the name (18 point) and change the style to bold. (Your software may not have the ability to retrieve all of the character returns in the text. Add hard returns if necessary.)
4. Save the document as DTP3.
5. Add the paragraph **Relevant course work** by importing the file COURSES and placing it beneath the paragraph in the education section. (Use the inserting text function while importing text, or place the text and then cut or move and paste it into the correct area.)
6. Change the section title **ACTIVITIES/AWARDS** to **HONORS, SCHOLARSHIPS.**

> **Hint** Headings, subheadings, and body text need different emphasis. Using different typeface sizes and weights accomplishes this.

7. Enhance the readability of this resume by changing all section headings to bold.
8. Save the file as DTP3.
9. Proof your work. Make any corrections or adjustments. Save again if necessary.
10. Print the file DTP3.

11. Proof the printed document. Make any corrections or adjustments. Print again if necessary. Save again if necessary.

13. Close the file.

> Complete the entire exercise before answering the review questions.

Review

1. What is the purpose of this document?

2. Who is the audience?

3. Is the layout appropriate for the audience and purpose?

4. Is your document centered vertically and horizontally?

5. What would you do to make the document more eye appealing?

6. What steps did you take to add the **Relevant course work** paragraph into the education section?

7. What steps did you use to center text?

8. What steps did you use to boldface text?

9. What is the advantage of sending a professional-looking resume to a prospective employer?

10. Why do you save your publication frequently?

PLAN 3

Michael R. Sass

P.O. Box 244 Cochrane, WI 54622 (608) 555-2327

OBJECTIVE

Instructing Physics, Math, and/or related fields.

EDUCATION

Bachelor of Science (Magna Cum Laude) - May 1991.
Winona State University.
Major: Physics (Electronics option), GPA 3.5/4.0.
Minor: Mathematics.

Relevant course work:
Optoelectronics, Electronics, Control Theory, Computer Organization, Microprocessor Electronics, Fortran, Pascal, BASIC, Statistics, Calculus.

HONORS, SCHOLARSHIPS

Dean's list, 13 quarters, Honors Program.
Alliss Scholarship - senior year.

EXPERIENCE

1989-1991 Computer Repair Technician.
Academic Computing Services, Winona State University, Winona, Minnesota.
Used computer skills for troubleshooting IBM PC's, Apple IIe's, and other personal computers.
Wired mainframe terminals.

1989-1991 Instructional Assistant.
Physics Department, Winona State University, Winona, Minnesota.
Position included setting up, dismantling, and supervising labs, tutoring students in physics courses, and maintaining and repairing equipment. Built new electronic equipment designed by faculty.

VOLUNTEER WORK

Sunday School Teacher.
Member of First Responders in Pepin, Wisconsin.
Member of Volunteer Fire Department in Pepin, Wisconsin.

INTERESTS

Bicycling, Golf, and Fishing.

REFERENCES

Available upon request.

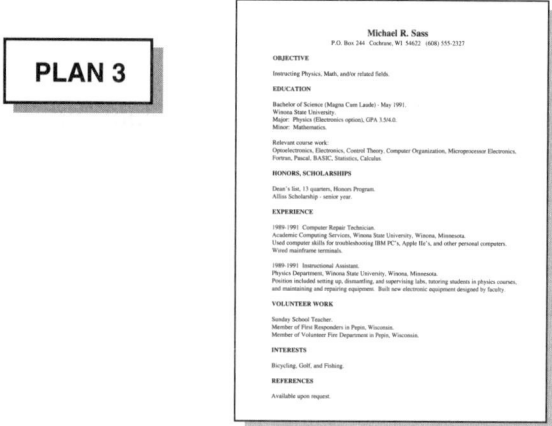

8½"
¾"
name 18 pt. bold
OBJECTIVE
EDUCATION
filename: COURSES
filename: RESUME3
HONORS, SCHOLARSHIPS
11"
1"
EXPERIENCE
¾"
VOLUNTEER WORK
or use default margins
REFERENCES
¾"

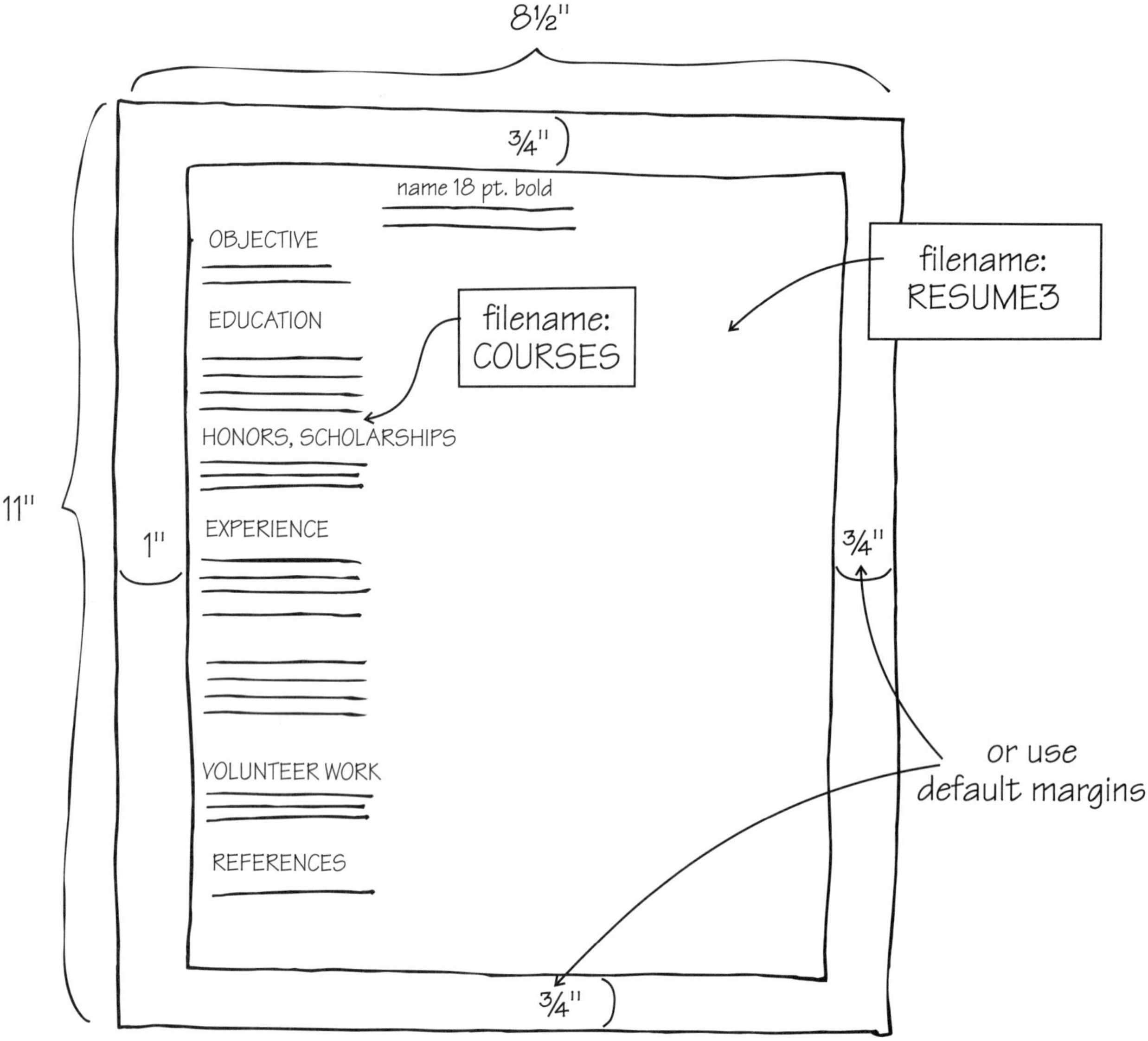

Name _____

Section _____ Date _____

Application 4 **Creating an Agenda**

Your supervisor has asked you to *desktop* an agenda for a professional organization. Agendas guide the progress of a meeting. They list the topics to be discussed so that all participants have a chance to prepare their remarks. The supervisor originally keyed the agenda, and you are now ready to edit and lay out the document.

1. Create a new one-page file in portrait (tall, or vertical) layout.
2. Set all margins at 2 inches. See plan 4.

> **Hint** Agendas are usually short and have extra white space to allow the participants to easily read and follow the items for the meeting. Therefore, larger margins are necessary to allow for note taking and readability.

3. Create a horizontal ruler guide 3 inches down from the top of the document if your software permits.
4. Import the text AGENDA4 so that it lines up below the 3-inch ruler guide (3 inches down from the top of the page) and next to the left margin guide.

> **Hint** Typefaces come in different sizes known as point size. Body copy would normally be anything from 9-point to 12-point type. Headings are larger for emphasis.

5. Create the heading as shown in plan 4 in any typeface (such as helvetica), 18-point bold at the top margin. Heading should read "Beta Chapter–Delta" Tentative Agenda, January, 199–.
6. Import the graphic BCDLOGO and place it above the top margin in the right-hand corner or place it above the heading in the right-hand corner.
7. Save the document as DTP4.

8. Spell check the document if your software is capable. (Error(s) is/are present. For all applications, use the spell check to help you proof the documents, but remember to proof as well.)
9. Proof your work. Make any corrections or adjustments. Save again if necessary.
10. Print the document.
11. Proof the printed document. Make any corrections or adjustments. Print again if necessary. Save again if necessary.
12. Close the file.

> Complete the entire exercise before answering the review questions.

Review

1. What is the purpose of this document?

2. Who is the audience?

3. Is the layout appropriate for the audience and purpose?

4. What could you do to make the document more eye appealing?

5. Proof the content of the agenda again.

    a. Are the items in sequence?

    b. Is there even spacing between items?

    c. What words were misspelled?

6. If your desktop publishing software does not contain a spell check option, how can you compensate?

   _____
   _____

7. Why is it important to proofread your publication more than once?

   _____
   _____

8. What special layout features do you need to apply to an agenda?

   _____
   _____

9. How many type families are available for use in your desktop publishing package?

   _____
   _____

10. What type families do(es) your printer(s) support?

    _____
    _____

11. What is the smallest point size? largest?

    _____
    _____

Creating an Agenda • 17

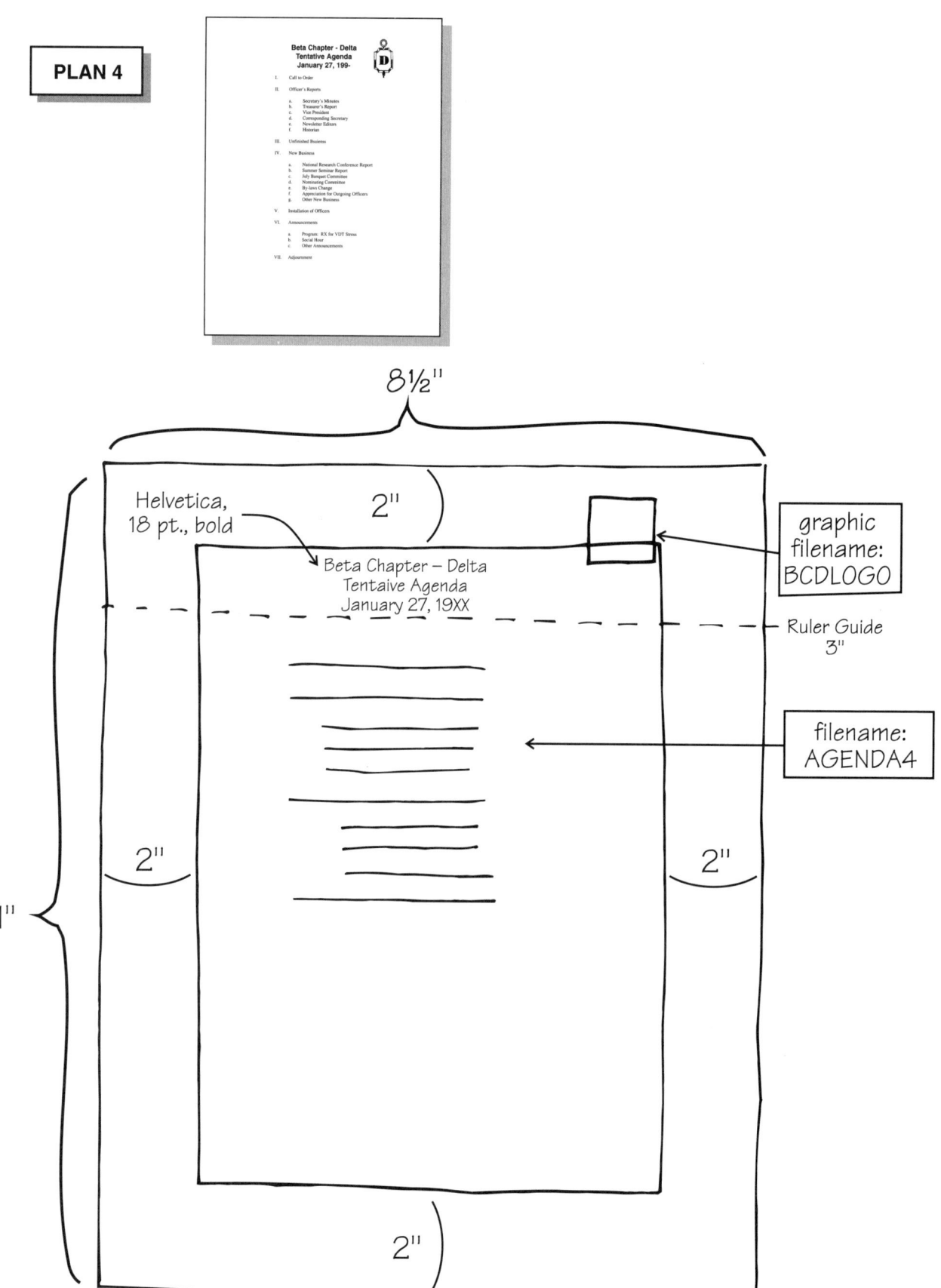

18 • **Creating an Agenda**

Name _____
Section _____ Date _____

Application 5 Creating a Newsletter

Beta Chapter–Delta (BCD) hired your firm to create its quarterly newsletter. You are in charge. Assume BCD has created the articles using word processing software and the masthead using graphics software. You are now ready to create a template that contains the correct margins and column settings. Then you will place the text and graphic (masthead) that were prepared previously. You will save the file with only the layout and masthead as a template to be used repeatedly. You will then add text to the newsletter for this issue and save the file as a document for this publication.

1. Create a new one-page file in portrait (tall, or vertical) layout. Refer to plan 5.

2. Set top margin at 3 inches and all other margins at 1 inch.

3. Create two columns or two text blocks that are equal in width with .25 inch between the two columns. (Some software will require you to flow the text from column 1 to column 2.)

4. Create a ruler guide .5 inch down from the top of the document if your software permits.

> **Hint** Sometimes when you import a graphic, it may not be placed correctly on the page. Depending on your software, you may have to delete the graphic and import it again or just use your tools to move the graphic into position.

5. Import the masthead BCD5. Place the masthead below the .5 inch ruler guide aligned with the left margin (or .5 inch down from the top of the page at the left margin). The masthead should span across both columns.

6. Add **March, 199–** below the masthead on the right side selecting a font to match the rest of the document.

7. Save this file as NEWSTEMP. (You may save the file as a template type if your software allows for this function.)

> **Hint** Templates serve as *dummy layouts* to be used repeatedly. Once you have created the general layout of a document, it can be used repeatedly as long as you save the skeleton layout (template) as one filename and the completed file with articles and headings under a different filename.

8. Import the text NEWS5A and place it at the upper left-hand corner of column 1.

> **Hint** When creating headlines, as a general rule, stick to the same typeface family throughout the document. Boldface type is authoritative. Italic provides emphasis. Bold and italic suggests action. Avoid underlining.

9. Change the size of the title of article NEWS5A to 18 point. Change the style of this title to boldface. You may need to add a hard return to avoid hyphenation. Check the bottom of column 1. Must you compensate for a widow?

> **Hint** *Widows* and *orphans* are short lines appearing alone at the top (orphan) or bottom (widow) of a page or column. Avoid widows and orphans by lengthening or shortening a text block so that a widow flows to the next column or an orphan remains in the column.

10. Flow the extra text from column 1 to column 2. Check the top of column 2. Must you compensate for an orphan?
11. Import the text NEWS5B and place it beneath the first article in column 2.
12. Change the size of the title of article NEWS5B. Use the same font and style that you used for the previous article title.
13. Save the document as DTP5. (Be careful that you do not save the document as NEWSTEMP since this is the newsletter template that you will use again next time you create this newsletter.)
14. Proof your work. Make any corrections or adjustments. Save again if necessary.
15. Print the document DTP5.
16. Proof the printed document. Make any corrections or adjustments. Save again if necessary. Print again if necessary.
17. Close the file.

> Complete the entire exercise before answering the review questions.

Review

1. What is the purpose of this document?
   _____
   _____

2. Who is the audience?
   _____
   _____

3. Is the layout appropriate for the audience and purpose?
   _____
   _____

4. How much white space frames your document?
   _____

5. How much white space surrounds your headlines?
   _____

   Do you need more? less?_____

6. Does your text line up evenly at the top of both columns?
   _____

7. What steps did you use to center the masthead horizontally?
   _____

8. Are your articles complete or is text at the end missing?
   _____

   If it is, adjust your text block so that all text appears.

9. What steps did you use to make text flow from one column to another?
   _____
   _____

10. Why did you save this newsletter once as NEWSTEMP and later as DTP5?
    _____
    _____

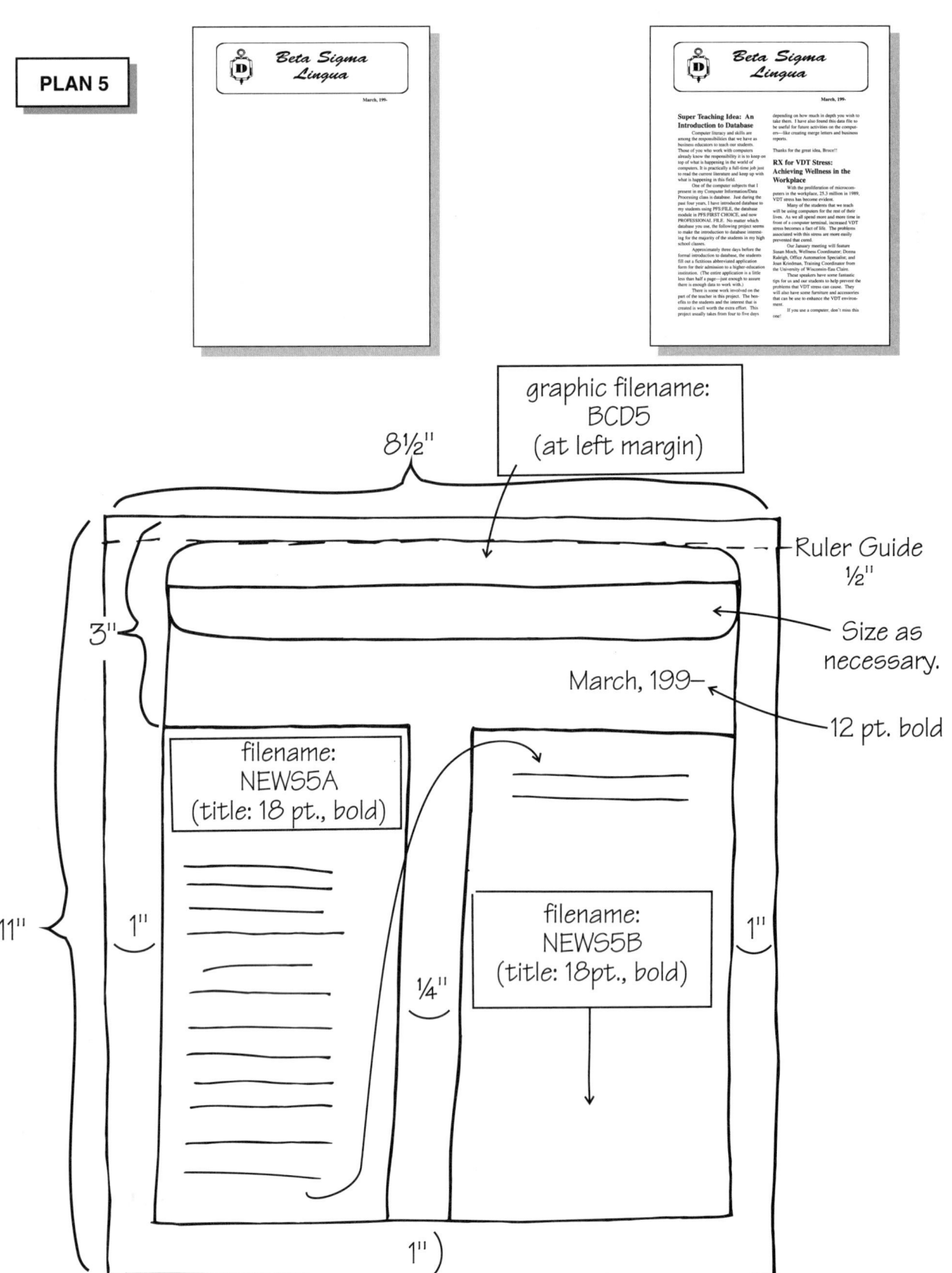

Unit 1
Performance Challenge

It is now the next quarter (3 months later), and you must create another newsletter for Beta Chapter–Delta. You will use the template document and import new text. Use the layout plan shown in figure U1.1 to create your document. General steps are provided for you.

1. Open the file NEWSTEMP.
2. Change the date below the banner to reflect the next quarter.
3. Import the first article, PCAGEND. Place it according to the plan in plan U1. Center the heading and change the first two lines to 18-point bold and the last two lines of the heading to 14-point bold type. The body text size is 10 point. (Edit for spacing in body of text.)
4. Import the second article, PCOFFIC. Place it according to the plan. The article is long enough to go to additional pages. Only lay out the first page. Create the heading at the beginning of the article. Change this heading to 18-point bold type. (See plan for other font changes.)
5. Adjust the text blocks at bottom margin for readability.
6. Proof the document. Spell check the document if possible.
7. Save the file as UNIT1PC.
8. Print UNIT1PC.
9. Proof the document. Make any necessary corrections or adjustments.
10. Save the file.
11. Print again if necessary.

PLAN U1

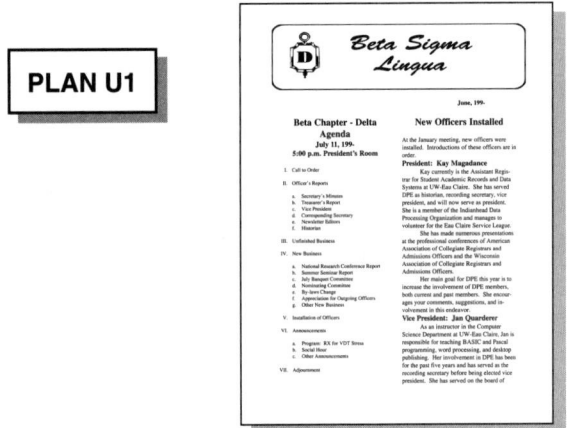

center
18 pt., bold
14 pt., bold

filename:
PCAGEND

10 pt.

June 199?

DPE Installs New Leadership — 18 pt. bold

filename:
PCOFFIC

President:

Vice President:

14 pt., bold

Body text
10 pt.

24 • Performance Challenge

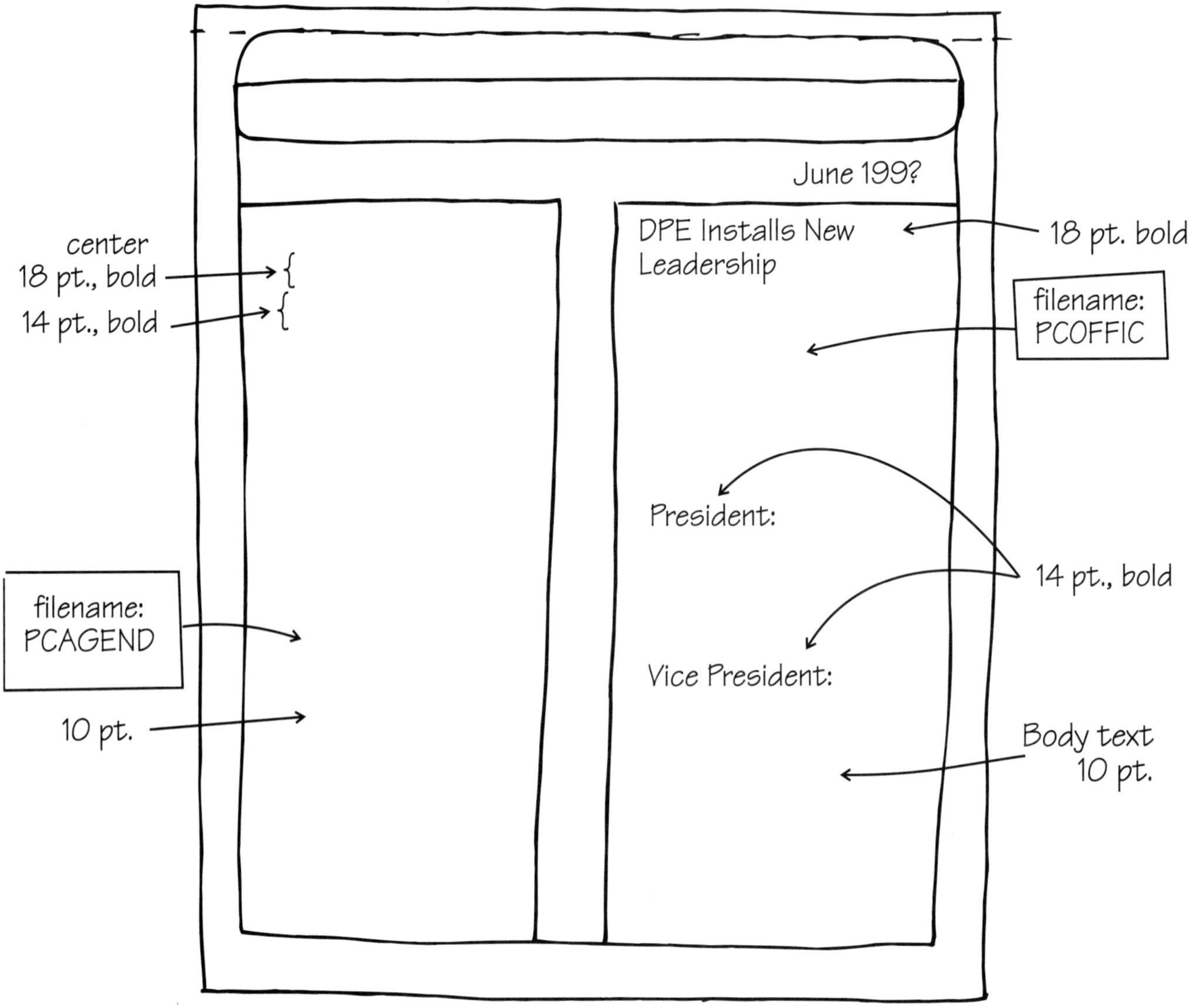

Unit 2
Enhancing Text and Page Layout

The applications in this unit apply a variety of techniques that will enhance the readability of the text. You will modify text justification, tabulation, typeface, size, style, kerning, and leading. To accomplish this you will create publications that require varied layouts such as one-column, two-column, three-column, bifold, and trifold layouts.

You will also use the search and replace, cut and paste, text rotation, style sheet, and copy-fitting features of your software.

Your finished documents will include a presentation document, company directory, product specification sheet, seminar advertisement (bifold), public relations sheet, poster, recruitment advertisement, survey, advertising flyer (trifold), and price lists. The Unit 2 Performance Challenge reviews the objectives presented in Applications 6 through 15.

Name _____

Section _____ Date _____

Application 6 Overhead Transparency

You are preparing a presentation on developing a new product for production for a customer. You will create an overhead transparency using your desktop publishing software. The transparency will be an outline of the department manager's presentation. The text has been created using word processing software.

1. Create a new one-page file in portrait or vertical layout. Set the top margin at 2 inches and all other margins at 1 inch.

2. Import the text GOALS6 and place it below the top margin and at the left margin. Change the size, font, and spacing of the text as indicated in plan 6. (You may have to set a hanging indent or left indent at .25" beyond the left margin.)

3. Save the presentation document as DTP6.

4. Move the information in the first bulleted item •**Sign...** below the information in the fifth bulleted item •**Southwestern....** Place .25 inch between the bullet and the first letter of text.

5. Search for all occurrences of the word **CA** and replace with the word **California.**

6. Save the file as DTP6.

7. Proof your work. Make any corrections or adjustments. Save again if necessary.

8. Print the document.

9. Proof the printed document. Make any corrections or adjustments. Print again if necessary. Save again if necessary.

10. Close the file.

> Complete the entire exercise before answering the review questions.

Review

1. What is the purpose of this presentation document?

2. Who is the audience?

3. Is the layout appropriate for the audience and purpose?

4. Can you give an example of when the search and replace feature would be useful?

5. If your desktop publishing software does not have the search and replace feature, how would you compensate?

6. What is the procedure for moving blocks of information?

7. What is the procedure for printing more than one copy of a page?

8. In your opinion, what changes would you recommend to your client to increase the readability of this overhead transparency?

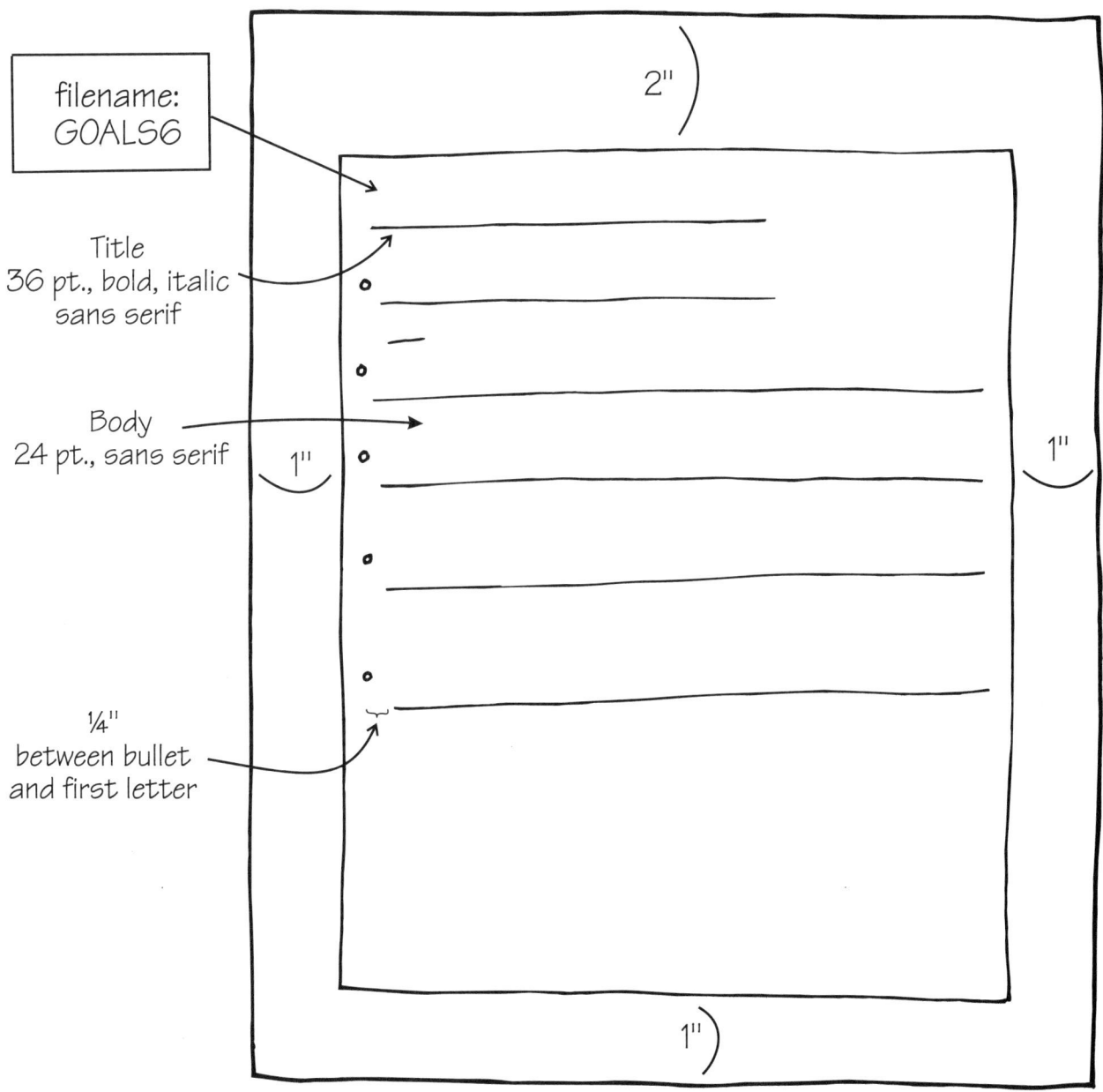

Name _____

Section _____ Date _____

Application 7 **Company Directory**

The people in your department constantly ask you and your supervisor for phone numbers of the other members of the company. Until now, you were the only ones who had access to this information. Because of the interruptions to your work, you discussed the problem with your supervisor. To correct the situation, your supervisor has asked you to create a company directory listing all employees and their office phone numbers. All the information should fit on one page.

1. Create a new file.
2. Set all margins to 1 inch.
3. If your software permits, create ruler guides .5, 1.5, and 2 inches down from the top of the document. Refer to plan 7.
4. Import the text INFO7 and place it at the left corner below the 2-inch ruler guide or 2 inches from the top of the page.
5. Set your tab settings to place the three columns of text about 2.5 inches apart.

Hint Serif typefaces have short, light lines or strokes extending from the upper and lower ends of the strokes of some letters. Serif typefaces are easier and less fatiguing to read when there is a large amount of small-sized copy presented. An example of a serif font is Times or Times Roman. Sans serif typefaces do not have these *feet* and are used for headings because of their ease of reading at larger sizes. An example of a sans serif font is Helvetica.

12-point Helvetica

24-point Helvetica

12-point Times

24-point Times

---

6. Change the text to a serif, 10-point typeface. The column headings and department names should be bold, 12-point serif type.
7. Save the document as DTP7.

8. Add the words **COMPANY DIRECTORY** in a sans serif, 24-point bold typeface 1.5 inches from the top of the page at the left margin (left justified).

9. Add the current date in a sans serif, 10-point bold typeface at the right margin (right justified) directly across from **COMPANY DIRECTORY.** Use the ruler guides, if your software permits, to help with alignment.

10. Save the document.

11. Proof your work. Make any changes or corrections. Save again if necessary.

12. Print DTP7.

13. Proof the printed document. Make corrections and print again if necessary.

14. Close the file.

> Complete the entire exercise before answering the review questions.

Review

1. What is the purpose of this document?

2. Who is the audience?

3. Is the layout appropriate for the audience and purpose?

4. What is the procedure for setting tabs?

5. What is the difference between a serif and a sans serif typeface?

6. What is the advantage of using a sans serif font?

   _____
   _____

7. What is the purpose of preparing a company directory and distributing it to all employees?

   _____
   _____

8. What procedure did you follow to enter the date at the right margin on the same line as **COMPANY DIRECTORY?**

   _____
   _____

PLAN 7

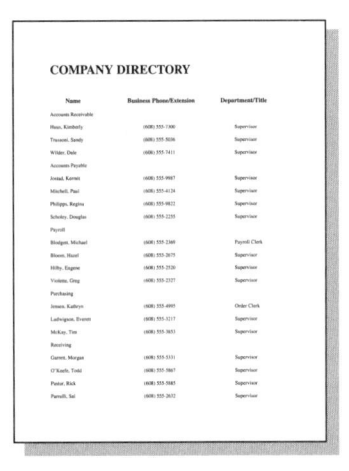

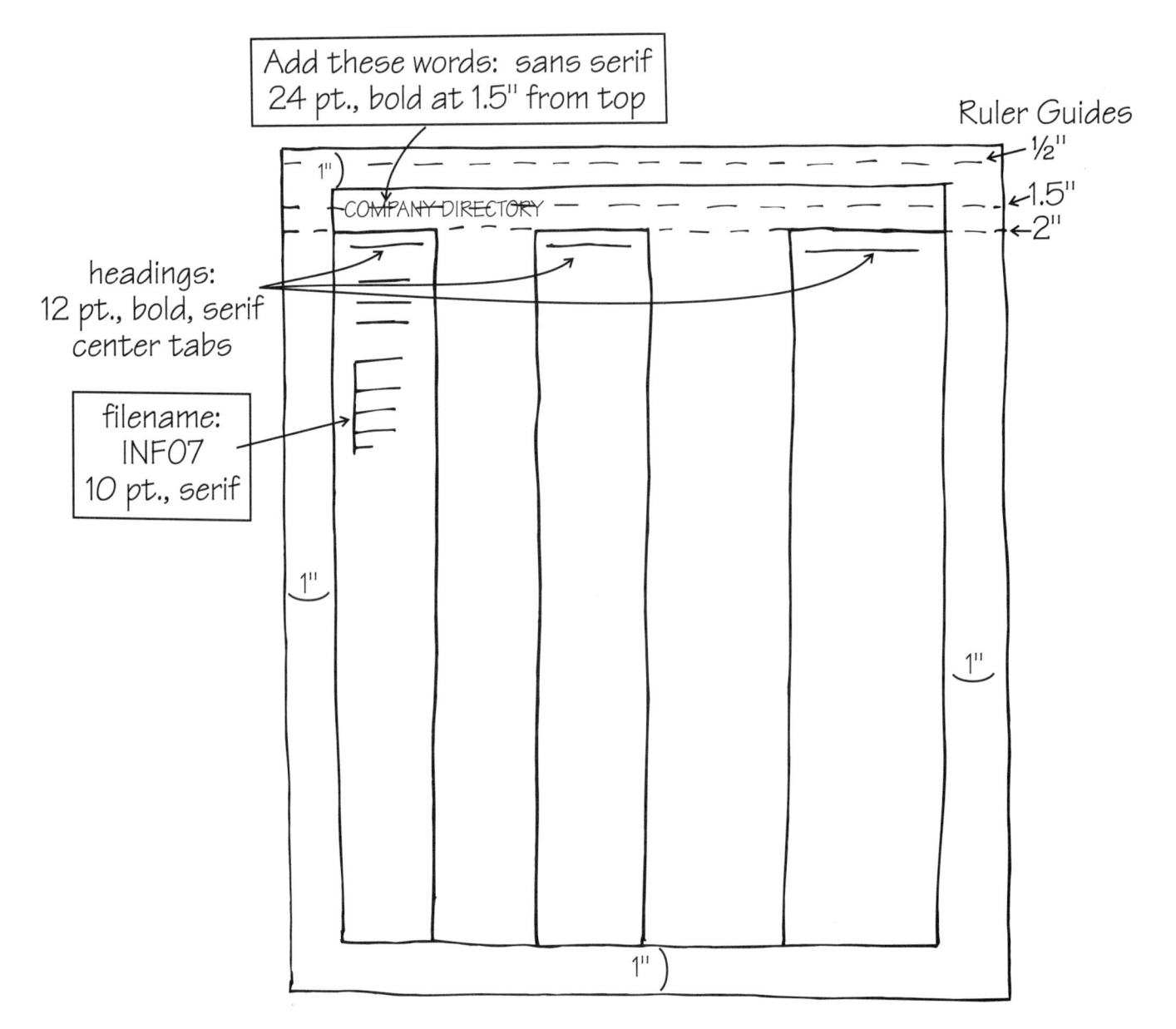

COMPANY DIRECTORY

Name	Business Phone/Extension	Department/Title
Accounts Receivable		
Buss, Kimberly	(608) 555-7300	Supervisor
Truscott, Sandy	(608) 555-5036	Supervisor
Wilder, Dale	(608) 555-7411	Supervisor
Accounts Payable		
Jostad, Kermit	(608) 555-9987	Supervisor
Mitchell, Paul	(608) 555-4124	Supervisor
Philipps, Regina	(608) 555-0022	Supervisor
Schisley, Douglas	(608) 555-2235	Supervisor
Payroll		
Blodgett, Michael	(608) 555-2368	Payroll Clerk
Bloom, Hazel	(608) 555-2675	Supervisor
Hilby, Eugene	(608) 555-2520	Supervisor
Victoria, Greg	(608) 555-2327	Supervisor
Purchasing		
Jensen, Kathryn	(608) 555-4995	Order Clerk
Ladwigson, Everett	(608) 555-1117	Supervisor
McKay, Tim	(608) 555-3653	Supervisor
Receiving		
Garrett, Morgan	(608) 555-5331	Supervisor
O'Keefe, Todd	(608) 555-5067	Supervisor
Pastor, Rick	(608) 555-3885	Supervisor
Parnell, Sal	(608) 555-2652	Supervisor

Add these words: sans serif 24 pt., bold at 1.5" from top

Ruler Guides
½"
1.5"
2"

headings: 12 pt., bold, serif center tabs

filename: INF07 10 pt., serif

1"
1"
1"
1"

Name _____
Section _____ Date _____

Application 8 **Product Specification Sheet**

Companies often need to provide product information to customers. The customers do not want an entire catalog; they are interested in only one product. Product specification sheets help both salespeople and customers become knowledgeable about a specific product. A product specification sheet for a new product must be created by this afternoon.

1. Create a new file.
2. Set the top margin at 1.5 inches and all other margins at 1 inch. Refer to plan 8.
3. Create two columns. Column 1 should be 2 inches wide. Column 2 should be 4 inches wide. There should be .5 inch between the columns.

Hint Paragraph spacing inserts the specified space either before or after each paragraph (return/enter code).

4. Import the text SPEC8C2 and place it at the upper left-hand corner of column 2. Insert an extra return as indicated in the plan after items 4, 10, and 16. Set tabs so the decimal points align properly and so the enumerated items are formatted in hanging indent format. Set paragraph spacing to .15" after each paragraph if necessary.
5. Save the document as DTP8.
6. Import the headline HEAD8. Place this headline in the area reserved for it above the columns in the margin. Change the text to 30 point, sans serif, bold.
7. Center the headline.
8. Save the document.
9. Create the rest of the information (as seen in plan 8) in column 1 in a larger type size (14 point) than the information in column 2. Use a serif, bold typeface.

10. Proof the document and spell check if available.
11. Save the document.
12. Print the document.

> Complete the entire exercise before answering the review questions.

Review

1. What is the purpose of this document?
   _____
   _____

2. Who is the audience?
   _____

3. Is the layout appropriate for the audience and purpose?
   _____

4. What makes this document eye appealing?
   _____
   _____

5. What font did you use for the headlines?
   _____

6. What steps did you use to align the information in the columns?
   _____

7. What changes would you make to enhance the visual appeal of this specification sheet?
   _____
   _____

8. What purpose does a product specification sheet serve?
   _____
   _____

9. What procedure did you follow to align the numbers at the decimal point?
   _____
   _____

10. What procedure did you follow to align the enumerated items in hanging indent format?
    _____

PLAN 8

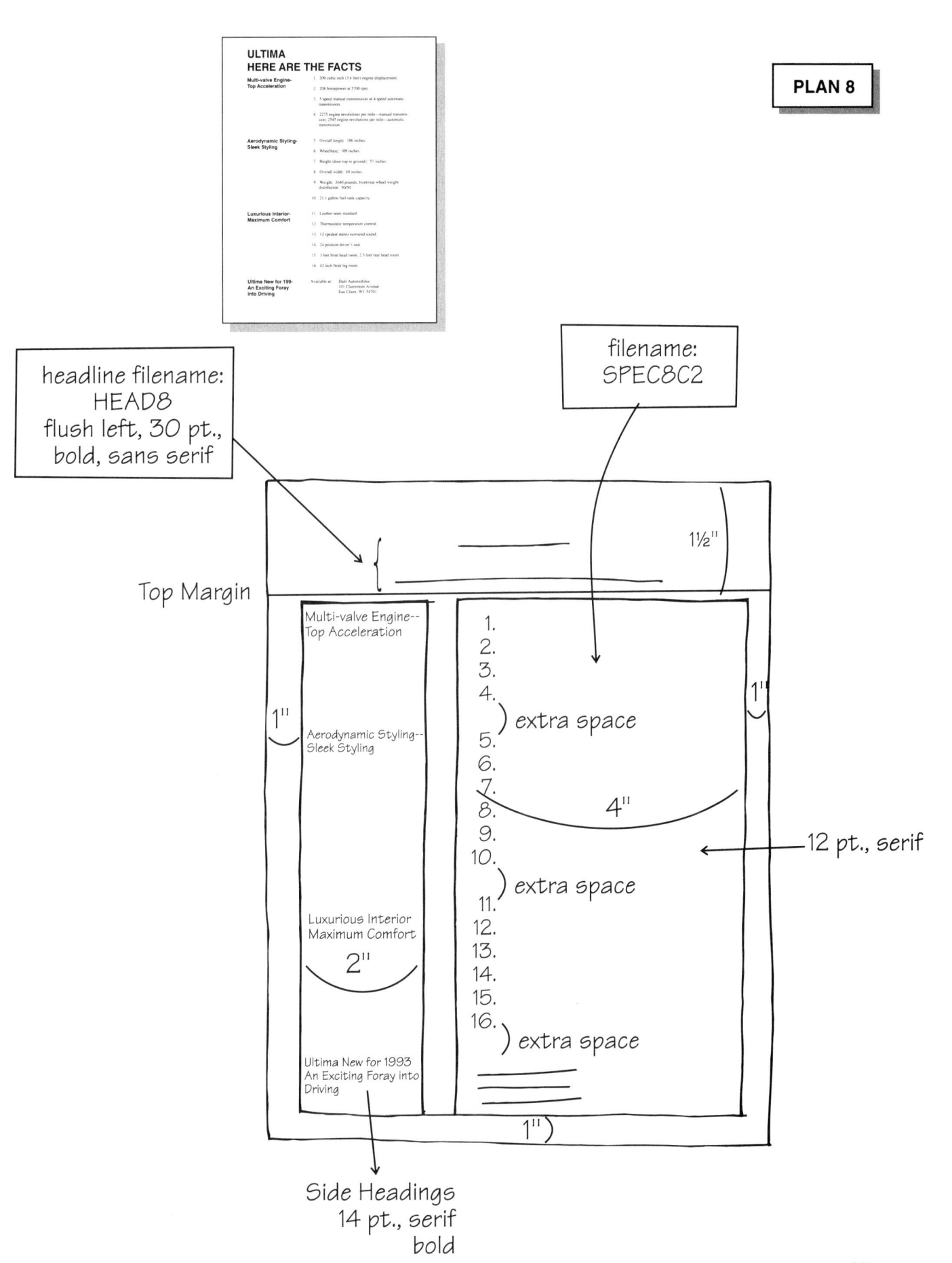

headline filename: HEAD8
flush left, 30 pt., bold, sans serif

filename: SPEC8C2

Top Margin: 1½"

Side margins: 1"
Bottom margin: 1"

Column width (right): 4"
Side headings column indent: 2"

Side Headings
14 pt., serif
bold

Body: 12 pt., serif

Side Headings:
- Multi-valve Engine-- Top Acceleration
- Aerodynamic Styling-- Sleek Styling
- Luxurious Interior Maximum Comfort
- Ultima New for 1993 An Exciting Foray into Driving

Items 1–16 with extra space after 4, 10, and 16.

Product Specification Sheet • 37

Name _____
Section _____ Date _____

Application 9 Seminar Advertisement (the Outside of a Bifold Brochure)

Event programs, seminar and workshop programs, menus, and invitations commonly use bifold brochures. This brochure is an advertisement for a seminar. In this activity, you will prepare the front and back cover (the outside page) of the brochure.

1. Create a new file. Choose landscape or horizontal as the orientation.

2. Set the margins at .5 inch.

3. Create ruler guides 1 inch and 3 inches down from the top of the document if your software permits.

4. Create two text blocks on the page with 1 inch between the blocks. This can be accomplished by creating two columns with a 1-inch gutter between the columns. See plan 9.

> **Hint** A style sheet is a collection of type specifications that have been given a name and can be applied to text. When you change a style on a global basis, every paragraph that was labeled with that style changes. This allows you to save the time and trouble of going through the text and reformatting it paragraph by paragraph.

5. Define a style sheet (or style) for spaced paragraphs. Specify that the type specifications be a serif font (like Times), 12 point, left justified, with .1 inch spacing before each paragraph. (You provide the style with a name.)

6. Define a style sheet for heading. Specify that the type specifications be a sans serif font (like Helvetica), 18 point, bold. (You provide the style with a name.)

7. Define a style sheet for subheading. Specify that the type specifications be a sans serif font (like Helvetica), 14 point, bold. (You provide the style with a name.)

8. Import the text for the cover, BROCOV9. Place it in column 2 below the 1-inch ruler guide (see plan 9).
9. Change the body text to the spaced paragraph style.
10. Change the heading to heading style and right justify it.
11. Change the subheading to subhead style and right justify it.
12. Create approximately .5 inch of white space between the heading and the subheading and between the subheading and the body copy. (Set paragraph spacing to .25 inch after the paragraph.)
13. Save the document as DTP9.

Hint Drop caps are used to introduce a column of text. A drop cap attracts attention and is often used in place of a graphic.

14. Create the drop cap (**L**) in the heading information in column 2 if your software permits.
15. Import the text for the back of the brochure, BROBACK9. Place it in column 1 below the 3-inch ruler guide. Use your style sheets to change the typeface so that it is the same as the body text on the cover (increase spacing between listed items).
16. Set a tab to change the format of the information regarding locations and dates to 2-column format.
17. The bulleted items should be formatted for hanging indent.
18. Save the brochure.
19. Proof your work. Make any changes or corrections. Add bold and/or italic styles to text if you feel the change in style would enhance the readability of the text. Save again if necessary.
20. Print DTP9.
21. Proof the printed document. Make corrections and print again if necessary.
22. Close the file.

> Complete the entire exercise before answering the review questions.

Review

1. What is the purpose of this document?

2. Who is the audience?

3. Is the layout appropriate for the audience and purpose?

4. What is the difference between landscape and portrait orientation?

5. What is the procedure for setting a specific amount of space for a paragraph indent?

6. What steps did you use to create the drop cap?

7. On the inside of this brochure, will page 1 be on the left or the right side of the layout?

8. What is the purpose of creating style sheets?

9. If your software does not have the capability of creating style sheets, how do you compensate?

PLAN 9

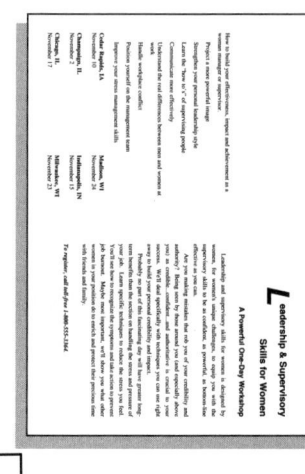

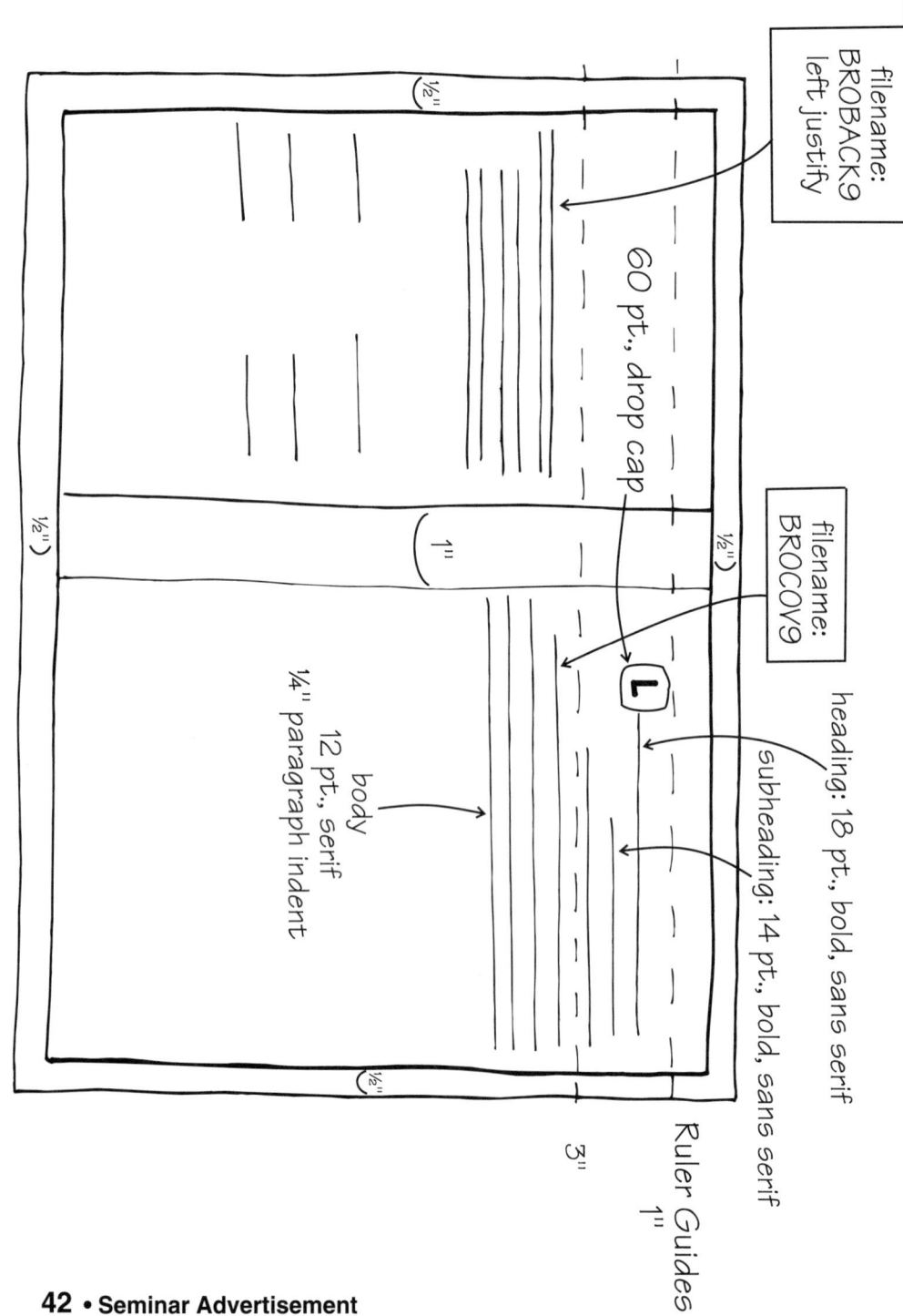

42 • Seminar Advertisement

Name _____
Section _____ Date _____

Application 10 Public Relations Sheet

Some businesses provide free information to their customers as a public service. The bridal registry department of a major department store would like you to create a sheet of wedding tips that they will give to their customers. Create this sheet.

1. Create a new file. Choose portrait or vertical as the orientation.
2. Set the top and bottom margins at 1 inch, the left and right margins at .5 inch. Check plan 10 to set ruler guide for title.
3. Create two columns with .25 inch between columns.
4. Import the text STYLE10 and place it .5 inch below the top margin in column 1. Format enumerations correctly.
5. Import the text EXPENS10 and place it below STYLE10. This text should flow to column 2.
6. Change all text to a serif, 10-point typeface.
7. Save the document as DTP10.

> **Hint** Most professional designers use one or two typefaces in a single document. You can enhance basic typefaces by using bold or italics while still maintaining a unified look. Using many different faces and type styles tends to distract the reader.

8. Change the heading of each article to boldface type.

> **Hint** Increasing the leading of a line increases the amount of white space below the line. The most common leading is to have 120% of the type size as the leading size. Altering the leading can render interesting visual effects as well as positive results for copyfitting. For example, if text does not fill the space you planned for it, increase the leading between the lines.

9. In the EXPENS10 text, change the subheadings to italics and increase the leading of the subheadings to 20 points.
10. In the STYLE10 text, adjust the tabs for appropriate enumerations.

11. Add the title **Tips for Weddings** in an appropriate typeface, style, size, and weight according to figure 10.1.
12. Save the file.
13. Proof your work. Make any changes or corrections. Save again if necessary.
14. Print DTP10.
15. Proof the printed document. Make corrections and print again if necessary.
16. Close the file.

> Complete the entire exercise before answering the review questions.

Review

1. What is the purpose of this document?
   _____
   _____

2. Who is the audience?
   _____
   _____

3. Is the layout appropriate for the audience and purpose?
   _____
   _____

4. What is leading?
   _____
   _____

5. What effect did increasing the leading in instruction 9 have on the text?
   _____
   _____

6. How is the automatic leading calculated in your software?
   _____
   _____

7. What typeface did you choose for the title and why?
   _____
   _____

PLAN 10

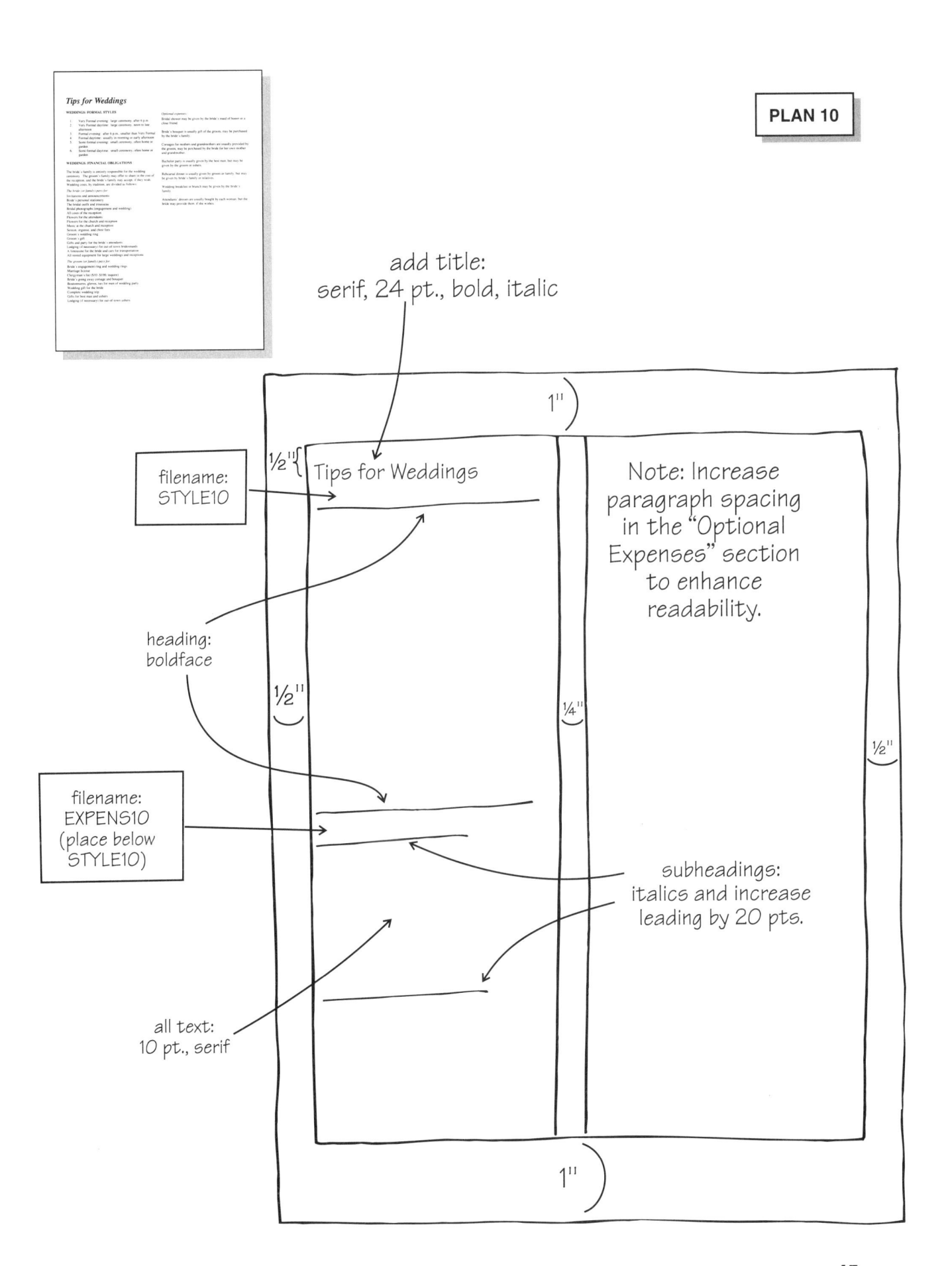

add title:
serif, 24 pt., bold, italic

filename:
STYLE10

Tips for Weddings

Note: Increase paragraph spacing in the "Optional Expenses" section to enhance readability.

heading:
boldface

filename:
EXPENS10
(place below STYLE10)

subheadings:
italics and increase leading by 20 pts.

all text:
10 pt., serif

Name _____
Section _____ Date _____

Application 11 Poster

Business organizations frequently use posters to advertise a product, seminar, workshop, or upcoming event. In this application you will create an informational poster.

1. Create a new file. Choose portrait.
2. Set the margins at 1 inch.
3. Create three columns of equal width.

> **Hint** A wall poster gets approximately 4 seconds of attention from passersby. It must make an immediate impact so it will be remembered.

4. Create text block A as shown in plan 11. Import the text POST11A and place it in the text block A. There may not be enough room for the existing text, but you will adjust the text block later.
5. Create three text blocks B, C, and D approximately 2 inches x 4 inches as shown in plan 11. Import the text POSTBX11 and place it in text block C. This text should be a serif, 18-point, bold, centered typeface.
6. Import the text POST11B into text block B. This text should flow to text block D. Right justify the text in text block B. Left justify the text in text block D. The text in these two blocks should be a serif, 14-point bold typeface with a .25-inch paragraph indent and .25-inch spacing after each paragraph.
7. Create text block E as shown in plan 11. Excess text from text block A should flow into text block E. The text in these two blocks should be a serif, 14-point, justified typeface. Do not indent the paragraphs.
8. Save the document as DTP11.

9. Create the drop caps (60 point, bold) indicated in plan 11 if possible. The drop cap in text block A helps tie the logo (nameplate at bottom of the page) to the body copy.
10. Adjust the leading of all text to fill all text blocks.
11. Save the document.
12. Create the nameplate on the bottom of the page. Rotate the text THE as illustrated in plan 11, if your software and printer are capable.
13. Add the text that is missing below the nameplate.
14. Save the document.
15. Proof your work. Make any changes or corrections. Save again if necessary.
16. Print DTP11.
17. Proof the printed document. Make corrections and print again if necessary.
18. Close the file.

> Complete the entire exercise before answering the review questions.

Review

1. What is the purpose of this document?

2. Who is the audience?

3. Is the layout appropriate for the audience and purpose?

4. What is the design effect of using drop caps in text?

5. What is the procedure for flowing text from column to column and why is it used?

6. What purpose does the left and right justification on this poster serve?

   _____

   _____

7. If your software allows you to rotate text, what is the procedure?

   _____

   _____

8. If your software does not rotate text, what could you do to compensate?

   _____

   _____

PLAN 11

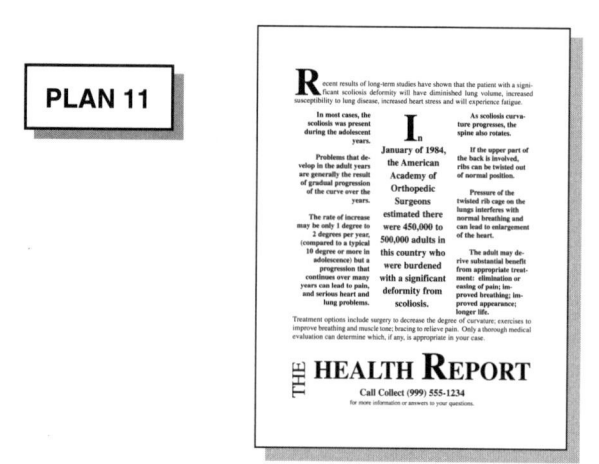

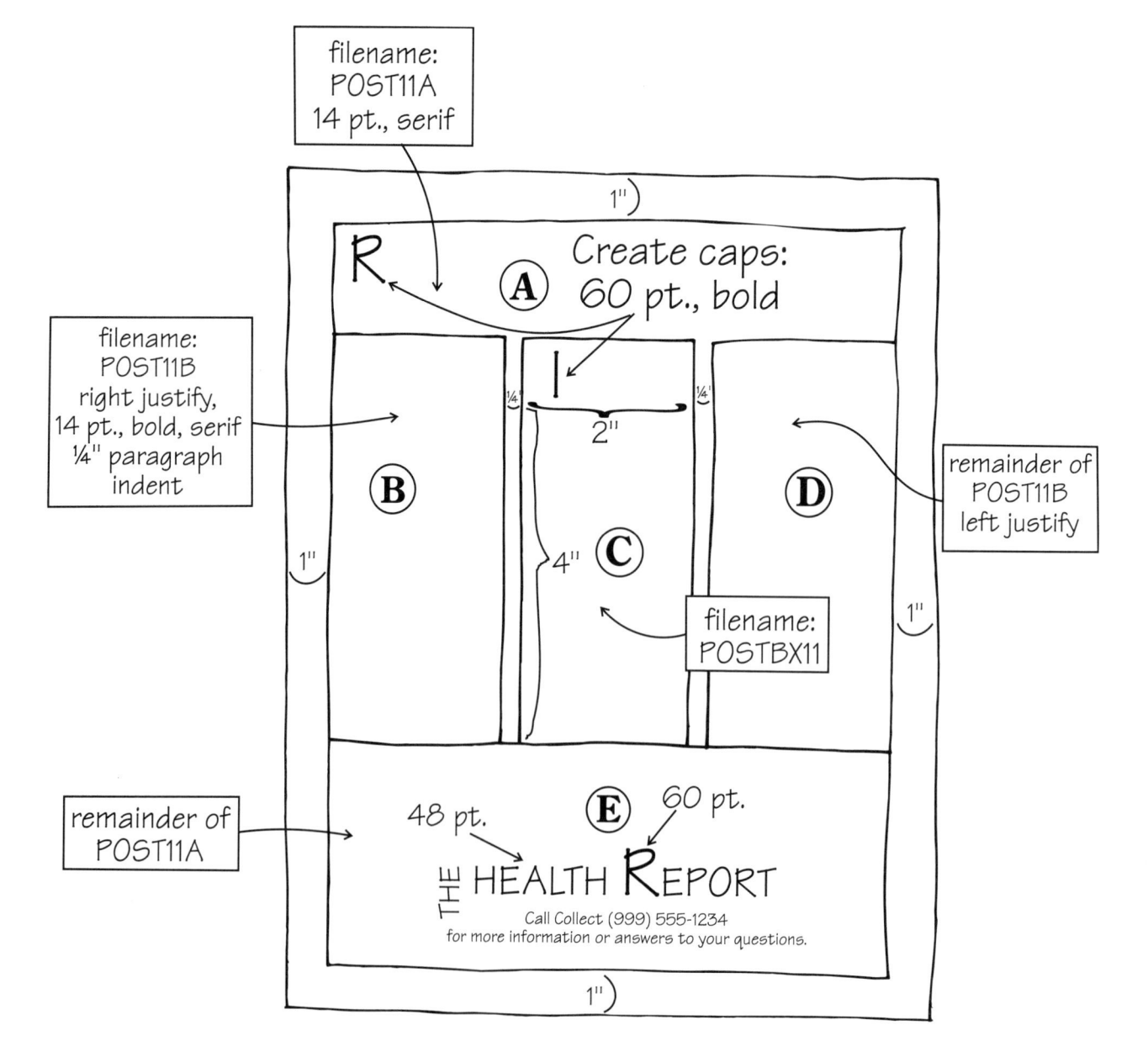

filename: POST11A
14 pt., serif

filename: POST11B
right justify,
14 pt., bold, serif
¼" paragraph indent

remainder of POST11A

Create caps:
60 pt., bold

1"

Ⓐ
Ⓑ
Ⓒ 4"
Ⓓ
Ⓔ

¼'   2"   ¼'

remainder of POST11B
left justify

filename: POSTBX11

48 pt.   60 pt.

THE HEALTH REPORT
Call Collect (999) 555-1234
for more information or answers to your questions.

1"

50 • Poster

Name _____

Section _____ Date _____

Application 12 Recruitment Advertisement

Organizations frequently create unique layouts for advertisements to attract possible applicants to their job openings. You are to prepare this recruitment piece, which will be placed in a newspaper (in reduced size). The ad also will appear as posters in the client's building and at job employment agencies.

1. Create a new file. Check plan 12 for layout orientation and margins.
2. Create two columns: make the first column 1.5 inches wide and the second column 5 inches wide. Put a .25-inch gutter between the columns.
3. Create horizontal ruler guides 2.5, 3, 3.5, and 7.5 inches below the top margin if your software permits.
4. Import the text TEXT12 and place it below the 3.5-inch ruler guide. Create a body copy style sheet using 12 point, serif type with a .25-inch paragraph indent. Change the text to body copy style using the style sheet. Add the specification that the body copy in this document be justified.

> **Hint** Kerning is the process of moving letters closer together. Kern headlines to eliminate some of the white space between letters that appear too far apart. Some of the letter pairs that need kerning are VA, WE, AT, TI, VE.

5. Create a text block that spans both columns and place it immediately below the top margin. Use the heading style to key **DIRECTOR OF,** enter, **FIELD EXPERIENCE.** Change the size of the type so the heading fills the space in the text block. Kern the letters that appear too far apart, bringing them in closer for readability. Make sure they appear equally balanced with the other letters in the heading.

6. Create a text block for the subheading in column 2 immediately below the heading. Use headline style to key **Starting Salary $24,000.** Adjust the size of the type so that the subheading fills the space in the text block. Kern if necessary.

7. Use the subhead style to key the text as shown in plan 12 below the 7.5-inch ruler guide in column 2. Increase the size by 4 points or to 18 points. Change the font to a serif font. Increase the type size of the line **Positions Available.**

8. Save the document as DTP12.

9. Proof your work. Make any changes or corrections. Save again if necessary.

10. Print DTP12.

11. Proof the printed document. Make corrections and print again if necessary.

12. Close the file.

> Complete the entire exercise before answering the review questions.

Review

1. What is the purpose of this document?

2. Who is the audience?

3. Is the layout appropriate for the audience and purpose?

4. What is the purpose of using kerning?

5. In addition to VA, WE, AT, TI, and VE, what other pairs of letters might need to be kerned if they appear in a headline?

6. What is the procedure for spanning text over more than one column?

   _____

   _____

7. What is the procedure for recalling a previously defined style sheet?

   _____

   _____

PLAN 12

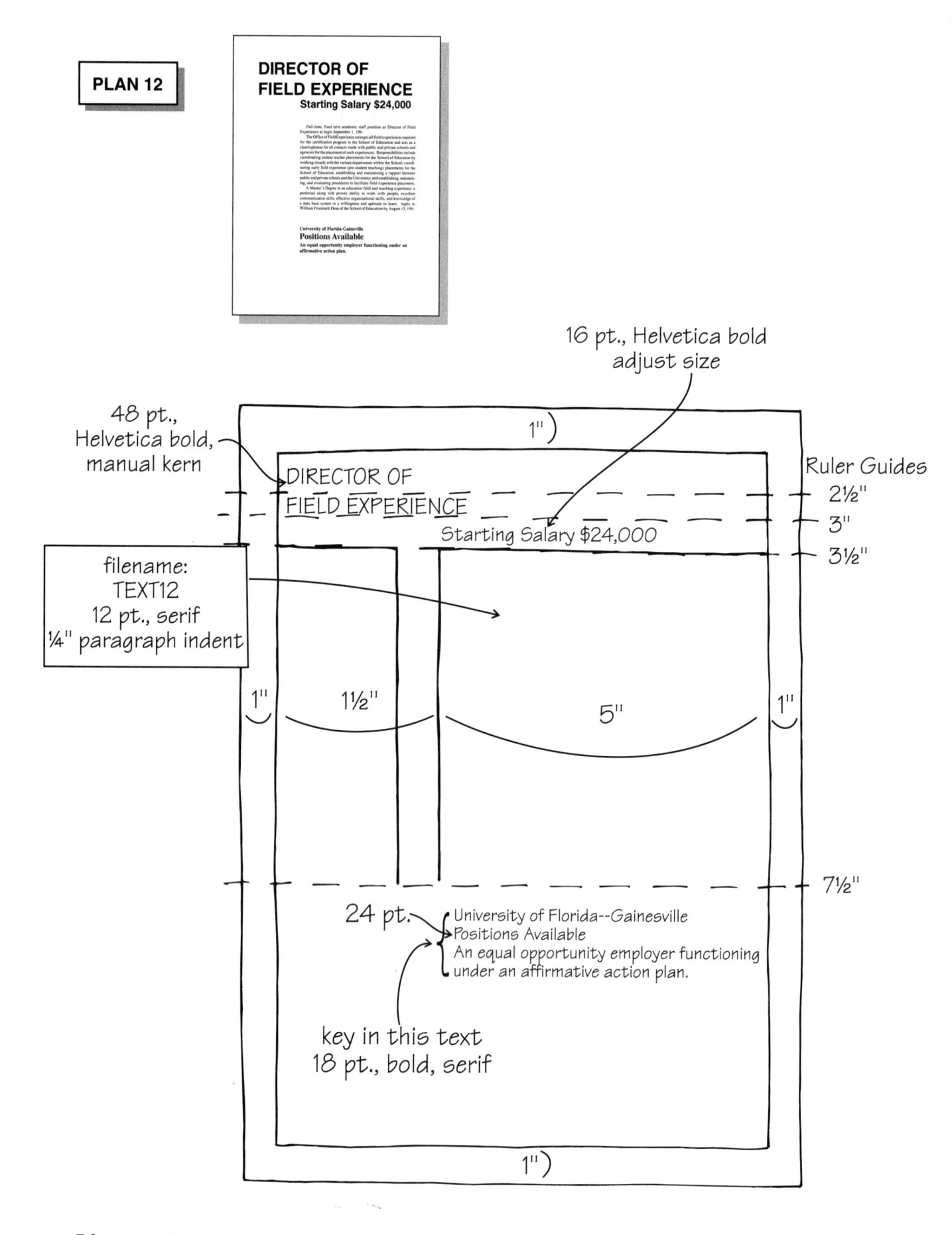

DIRECTOR OF FIELD EXPERIENCE
Starting Salary $24,000

48 pt., Helvetica bold, manual kern → DIRECTOR OF FIELD EXPERIENCE

16 pt., Helvetica bold adjust size → Starting Salary $24,000

Ruler Guides
- 2½"
- 3"
- 3½"
- 7½"

filename: TEXT12
12 pt., serif
¼" paragraph indent

Margins: 1" top, 1" bottom, 1" left (with 1½" inner), 1" right; text width 5"

24 pt.
- University of Florida--Gainesville
- **Positions Available**
- An equal opportunity employer functioning under an affirmative action plan.

key in this text
18 pt., bold, serif

54 • Recruitment Advertisement

Name _____

Section _____ Date _____

Application 13 **Survey**

People who work in research and development create surveys (questionnaires) to analyze the market and help determine what type of products their company will develop. Surveys are tools to gather information quickly from prospective buyers. They should be short and to the point with the use of as many check-off items as possible so that people can quickly complete them. You are to create a survey from the keyed information and enhance it so that is has a professional appearance.

1. Create a new file. Set margins at .5 inch.
2. From the margin, create three columns with .25-inch gutters. The second column should begin at 2.5 inches and the third column should begin at 4.25 inches.
3. Import the text SRVEY13A and place it in column 2. It should span columns 2 and 3.
4. Change the typeface of the heading to a sans serif, 36-point, bold typeface. Edit the editor's name and title to italic and right justified. The remainder of the text should be body copy style with a paragraph indention of 0.
5. Import the text SRVEY13B and place it according to plan 13. Adjust the spacing for readability.
6. Add the check boxes in front of each topic if that option is available. If you do not have a typeface that contains a box symbol, key in a three-character line.
7. Save the document as DTP13.
8. Add the section headings to the left of the topics in column 1. They should be a sans serif, 14-point, bold typeface and should be right justified.
9. Import the text SRVEY13C and place it according to the plan.
10. Add the return address in the lower left corner of the document.
11. Save the document.

12. Proof your work. Make any changes or corrections. Save again if necessary.
13. Print DTP13.
14. Proof the printed document. Make corrections and print again if necessary.
15. Close the file.

> Complete the entire exercise before answering the review questions.

Review

1. What is the purpose of surveys?

   _____
   _____

2. Who is the audience?

   _____
   _____

3. Is the layout appropriate for the audience and purpose?

   _____
   _____

4. What layout considerations must you apply when creating a survey?

   _____
   _____

5. Why are check-off boxes so prevalent in surveys?

   _____
   _____

6. Now that the survey is completed, do you think it could be easily filled out? Why or why not?

   _____
   _____

7. What layout changes would you make to this survey to enhance the readability?

   _____
   _____

PLAN 13

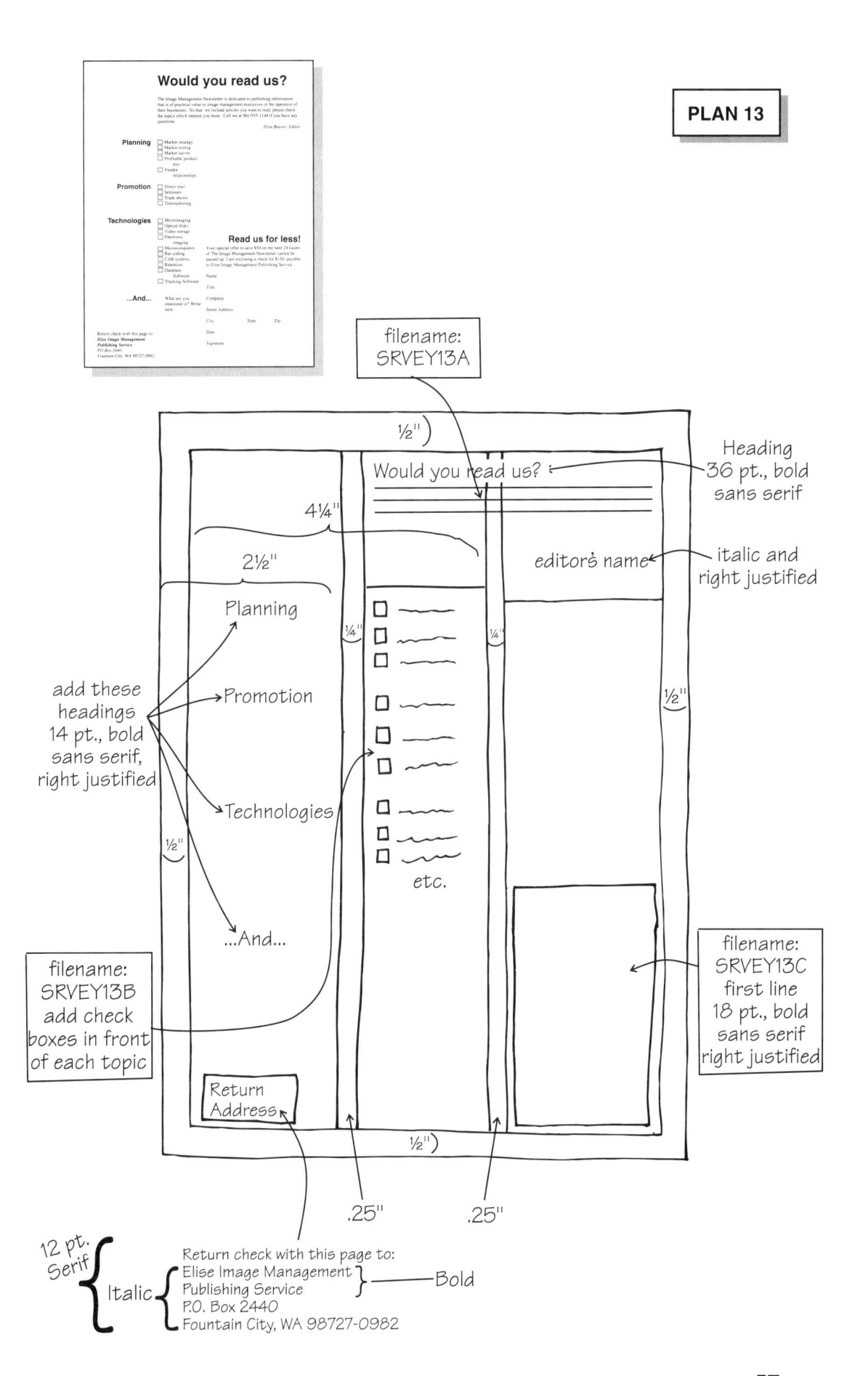

filename: SRVEY13A

Would you read us?

Heading 36 pt., bold sans serif

editor's name — italic and right justified

½"
4¼"
2½"
¼"
¼"
½"

Planning

add these headings 14 pt., bold sans serif, right justified

Promotion

Technologies

...And...

etc.

½"

filename: SRVEY13B add check boxes in front of each topic

Return Address

filename: SRVEY13C first line 18 pt., bold sans serif right justified

½")
.25" .25"

12 pt. Serif — Italic
Return check with this page to: — Bold
Elise Image Management
Publishing Service
P.O. Box 2440
Fountain City, WA 98727-0982

Survey • 57

Name _____

Section _____ Date _____

Application 14 **Advertising Flyer—Trifold Inside**

Another popular advertising tool is the trifold flyer. As with the bifold brochure, you can create a multitude of documents in this layout. For example, trifold flyers can be used to inform patients of new medical procedures or safety procedures. They also can be used to promote a seminar or workshop. Much planning must be completed to ensure that you are placing the information in the correct column, particularly on the outside of a trifold flyer. In this application, you will create the inside of a trifold flyer.

1. Create a new file. (Note: Use custom paper, 8½ inches x 14 inches.) See plan 14 for layout specifications.
2. Import the text ITM14-1 and place it at the top of column 1. Import the text ITM14-2 through ITM14-9, placing each below the previously imported text. Leave approximately .5 inch of white space between each text block. Format the text according to plan 14 using all columns.

> **Hint** By placing each item separately, you have more control over where the items will go on each page.

3. Save this document as DTP14.
4. Make each text block narrower to allow space for a graphic to the left of each column. Reserve about 1.5" on the left side of each column.
5. Change the size of the body text so that three items appear in each column. Choose an appropriate typeface and style. Change the format to include a hanging indent so the item number appears to the left of the paragraph as shown in the plan. When you have found an appropriate size, typeface, style, and format, define a style sheet named *hanging* that incorporates these specifications. Change all text to the hanging style.

6. Save the document.
7. Proof your work. Make any changes or corrections. Save again if necessary.
8. Print DTP14.

> **Hint** If your printer does not accept 8.5" x 14" paper, you will have to print the document in sections, or tiles. Choose the auto tile option when printing. This option divides your publication into section that can be assembled for the final product. You may also be able to request crop marks. These marks assist you when assembling the tiles and trimming edges. Or, you may scale the document, printing at 75% to fit on an 8.5" by 11" sheet of paper.

9. Proof the printed document. Make corrections and print again if necessary.
10. Close the file.

> Complete the entire exercise before answering the review questions.

Review

1. What is the purpose of this document?
   _____
   _____

2. Who is the audience?
   _____
   _____

3. Is the layout appropriate for the audience and purpose?
   _____
   _____

4. What is the process to adjust the width of text blocks?
   _____
   _____

5. For what types of publications are trifold flyers best suited?
   _____
   _____

PLAN 14

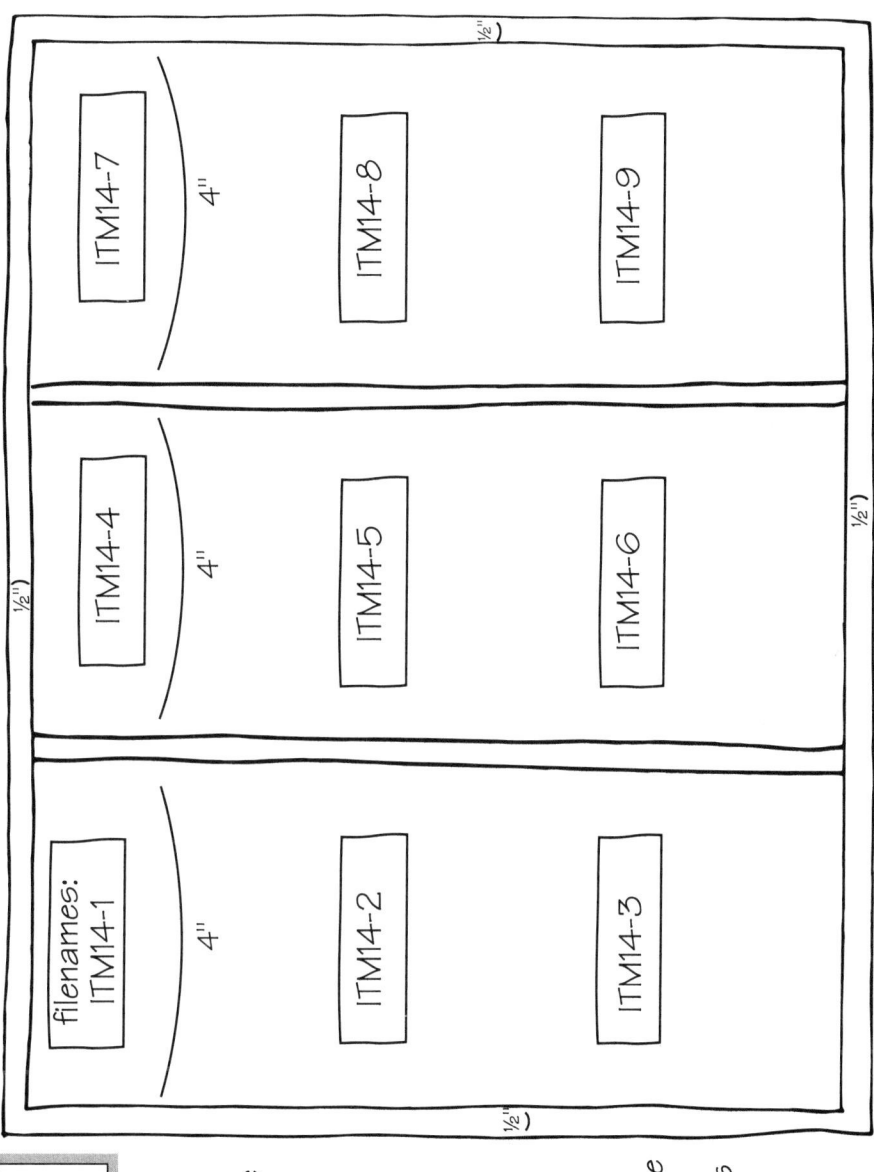

landscape 8½" x 14"

½")

½")

½")

ITM14-1 (filenames)	ITM14-4	ITM14-7
4"	4"	4"
ITM14-2	ITM14-5	ITM14-8
ITM14-3	ITM14-6	ITM14-9

choose appropriate font size and style

leave ½" white space between text blocks

Advertising Flyer—Trifold Inside • 61

Name _____

Section _____ Date _____

Application 15 Price List

Customers often ask for pricing information. Price lists allow information updates without the expensive cost of a catalog. They are easier and less costly to mail as well. With price lists, there are usually many columns of information as well as alignment factors to consider. Be sure you watch for this in your layout of the following price list.

1. Create a new file. Choose portrait.
2. Set all margins at .75 inch.
3. Create horizontal ruler guides at 1.5 and 2 inches down from the top of the document if your software permits.
4. Create three columns with .25 inch between. Column 1 should end at 2.75 inches; column 2 should end at 4 inches.
5. Import the text for the price list PRCLST15. Place it below the 2-inch horizontal ruler guide in column 3. See plan 15.

> **Hint** Align prices at the decimal point. If your software permits, set a decimal tab for the pricing column.

6. Change the body copy to a serif, 11-point, left-justified typeface. Set a left tab at 1 inch and a decimal tab at 3.5 inches. Reformat all part numbers in boldface if they are not already.
7. Change the column headings to 14 point, bold. Set one left tab at 1 inch and another at 3.25 inches.
8. Save the document as DTP15.
9. If necessary, create white space between each item in the list so that they are evenly spaced.
10. Create the text that is missing at the top of the document in an appropriate typeface.
11. Create the section headings in an appropriate typeface to draw attention to the headings.

12. Save the price list.
13. Proof your work. Make any changes or corrections. Save again if necessary.
14. Print DTP15.
15. Proof the printed document. Make corrections and print again if necessary.
16. Close the file.

> Complete the entire exercise before answering the review questions.

Review

1. What is the purpose of this document?

2. Who is the audience?

3. Is the layout appropriate for the audience and purpose?

4. What must you do to ensure proper alignment of numbers?

5. What procedure do you use to set tabs? What types of tabs are you able to set? What is the function of each type of tab?

6. Is the white space even on the price list?

7. What changes would you make to the price list to make it more effective?

PLAN 15

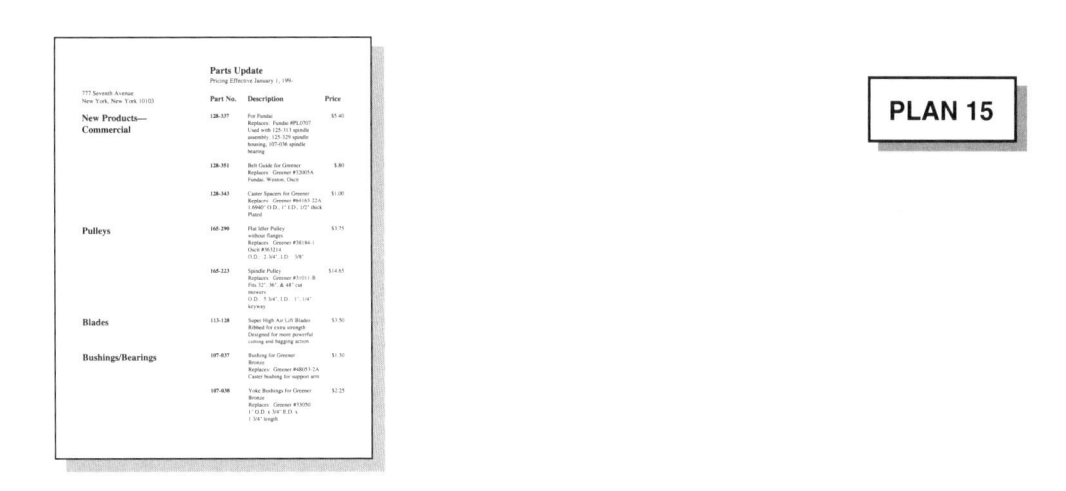

Sample layout (Parts Update)

777 Seventh Avenue
New York, New York 10103

Parts Update
Pricing Effective January 1, 199–

	Part No.	Description	Price
New Products—Commercial	128-337	For Fundat Replaces: Fundat #PL0707 Used with 125-313 spindle assembly, 125-329 spindle housing, 107-036 spindle bearing	$5.40
	128-351	Belt Guide for Greener Replaces: Greener #12005A Fundat, Weston, Osco	$.80
	128-343	Caster Spacers for Greener Replaces: Greener #64163-22A 1.6940" O.D., 1" I.D., 1/2" thick Plated	$1.00
Pulleys	165-299	Flat Idler Pulley without flanges Replaces: Greener #38184-1 Osco #38321-4 O.D., 2 3/4", I.D. 3/8"	$3.75
	165-223	Spindle Pulley Replaces: Greener #31011-B Fits 32", 36", & 48" cut mowers O.D., 5 3/4", I.D. 1", 1/4" keyway	$14.65
Blades	113-128	Super High Air Lift Blades Ribbed for extra strength Designed for more powerful cutting and bagging action	$3.50
Bushings/Bearings	107-037	Bushing for Greener Bronze Replaces: Greener #48053-2A Caster bushing for support arm	$1.30
	107-038	Yoke Bushings for Greener Bronze Replaces: Greener #33050 1" O.D. x 3/4" R.D. x 1 3/4" length	$2.25

Layout specifications

- 18 pt., bold (only top line)
- 12 pt.
- Ruler Guides
- 3/4" (top margin)
- 1½"
- 2"
- 12 pt.
- 777 Seventh Avenue, New York, New York, 10103
- Parts Update / Pricing Effective January 1, 199–
- Heading (14 pt., bold)
- 2¾" ¼"
- New Products—Commercial
- 4"
- Part numbers 11 pt., bold
- filename: PRCLST15
- body text 11 pt., serif
- Add headings: Pulleys, Blades, Bushings/Bearings
- 3/4"
- 3/4"
- tabs at 1" and 3½" from this column margin
- 3/4" (bottom margin)

Price List • 65

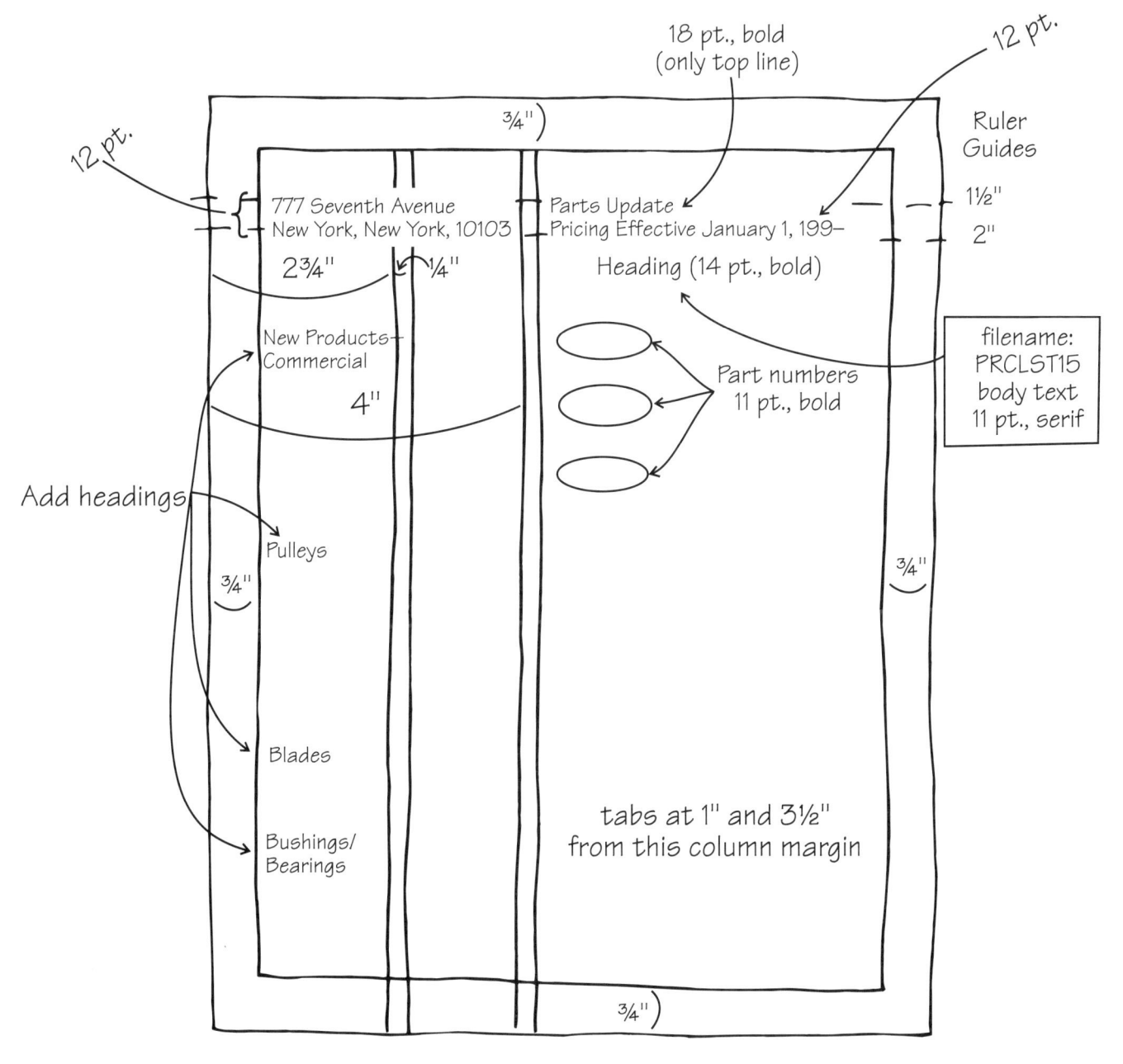

Unit 2
Performance Challenge

A local computer software and accessories wholesaler would like your firm to create a new layout for its catalog. Initially, you will create only one page.

1. Open a new file.
2. Import PC2PRIC. Place it according to plan U2.

> **Hint** Paragraph spacing inserts the specified space either before or after each paragraph (return/enter code). In this particular file, the same effect could be accomplished by specifying 18-point leading, which inserts extra space between each line of a paragraph as well as between paragraphs.

3. Change the paragraph spacing to .075 inch.
4. Change the size of the text so all text fits on the page.
5. Add the section headings using a heading style sheet.
6. Add the heading **PRICE LIST**. Change the size so that it fills column 2.
7. Add the company name **Warehouse** at both the top and bottom of column 1.
8. Add the address at the bottom of column 2.
9. Proof the document. Spell check the document if possible.
10. Save the file as UNIT2PC.
11. Print UNIT2PC.
12. Proof the document. Make any necessary corrections or adjustments.
13. Save the file.
14. Print again if necessary.

PLAN U2

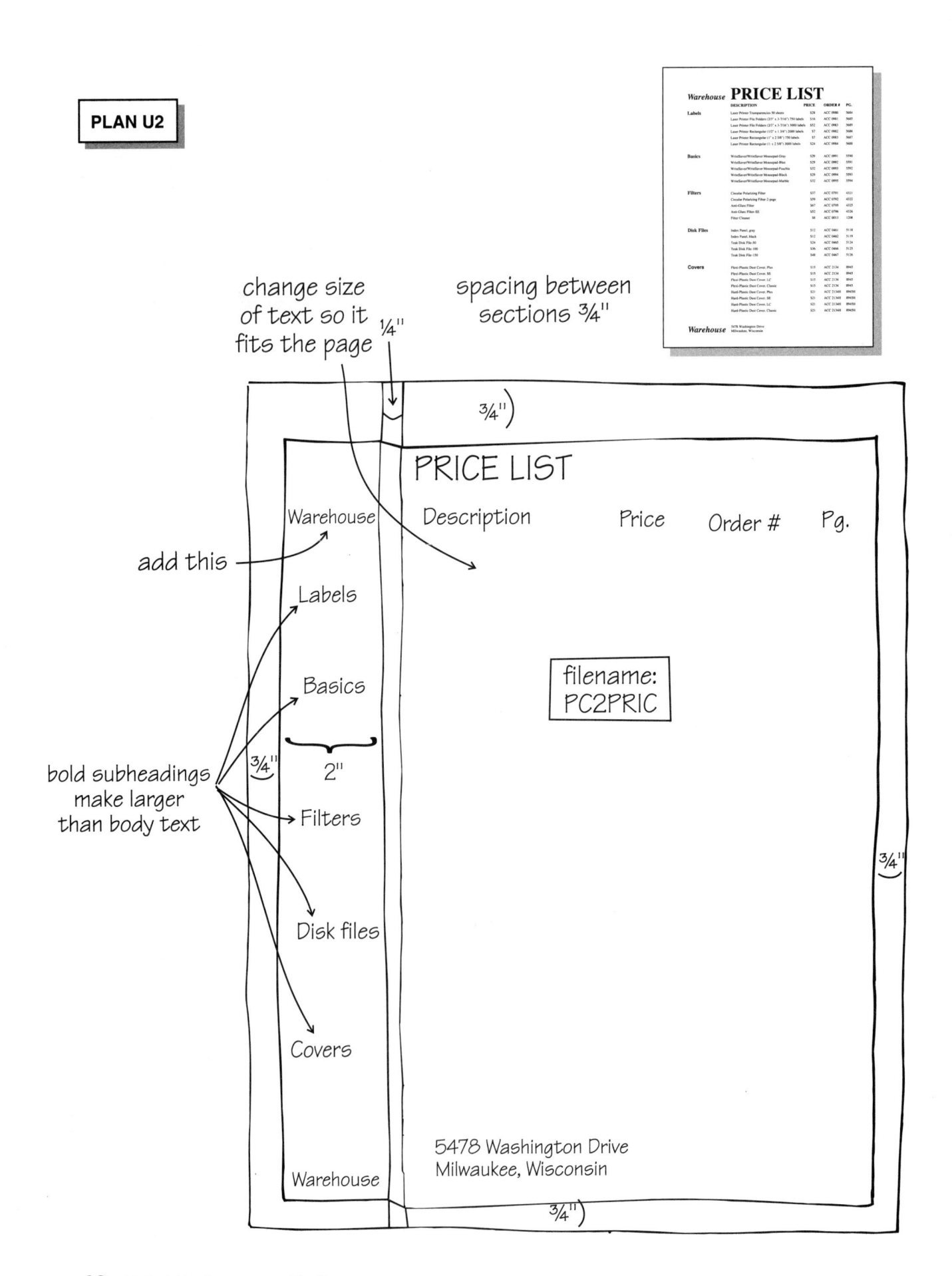

change size of text so it fits the page ¼"

spacing between sections ¾"

Warehouse PRICE LIST
(sample price list thumbnail)

¾"

PRICE LIST

Warehouse — Description — Price — Order # — Pg.

add this → Warehouse

Labels

Basics

bold subheadings make larger than body text

¾" { 2" }

Filters

filename: PC2PRIC

Disk files

Covers

¾"

5478 Washington Drive
Milwaukee, Wisconsin

Warehouse

¾"

Unit 3
Enhancing Publications with Graphics

The applications in this unit apply a variety of techniques that will enhance the visual appeal of the documents by adding graphic elements such as lines, boxes, scanned images and images created using paint or draw software packages. You will modify graphic elements through scaling, stretching, changing density, and changing color.

You will use the layering, text wrap, and graphic drawing features of your software. You will also create a document that is larger than legal size and may require printing the document in sections to be assembled manually.

Your finished documents will include a presentation document, company directory, product specification sheet, seminar advertisement (bifold), public relations sheet, poster, recruitment advertisement, survey, advertising flyer (trifold), price list, promotional flyer, newsletters, college brochure, resume, brochure with spot color, and organization chart. Unit 3 Performance Challenge reviews the objectives presented in Application 16 through Application 31.

Application 16 through Application 24 use the files you created in Application 7 through Application 15, DTP7 through DTP15, respectively. You will be enhancing Applications 7 through 15 by adding graphic elements to the documents.

Name _____

Section _____ Date _____

Application 16 Company Directory with Logo

Building on the company directory you started in application 7, add the company logo along with basic lines or rules to enhance the look of the document.

1. Open the file DTP7.

> **Hint** There are 72 points in 1 inch. Therefore, a 2-point line is 1/36 of an inch wide.

2. Add the 2-point horizontal line and the 1-point lines shown in plan 16.

> **Hint** Cropping is the process of making the graphic area smaller by trimming the unwanted portions of a graphic. This allows the designer to "cut" out part of the graphic or picture and only allow a certain portion of the picture to appear.

3. Import the graphic DIRLGO16 and place it above the top margin even with the left margin. You may have to crop and resize the graphic and move it into the correct position after importing it.
4. Save the publication as DTP16.
5. Proof your work. Make any changes or corrections. Save again if necessary.
6. Print DTP16.
7. Proof the printed document. Make corrections and print again if necessary.
8. Close the file.

> Complete the entire exercise before answering the review questions.

Review

1. What is the procedure for cropping a graphic?

   _____

   _____

2. What is the procedure for repositioning a graphic?

   _____

   _____

3. Does the addition of graphics improve the quality of the document? Why or why not?

   _____

   _____

   _____

   _____

PLAN 16

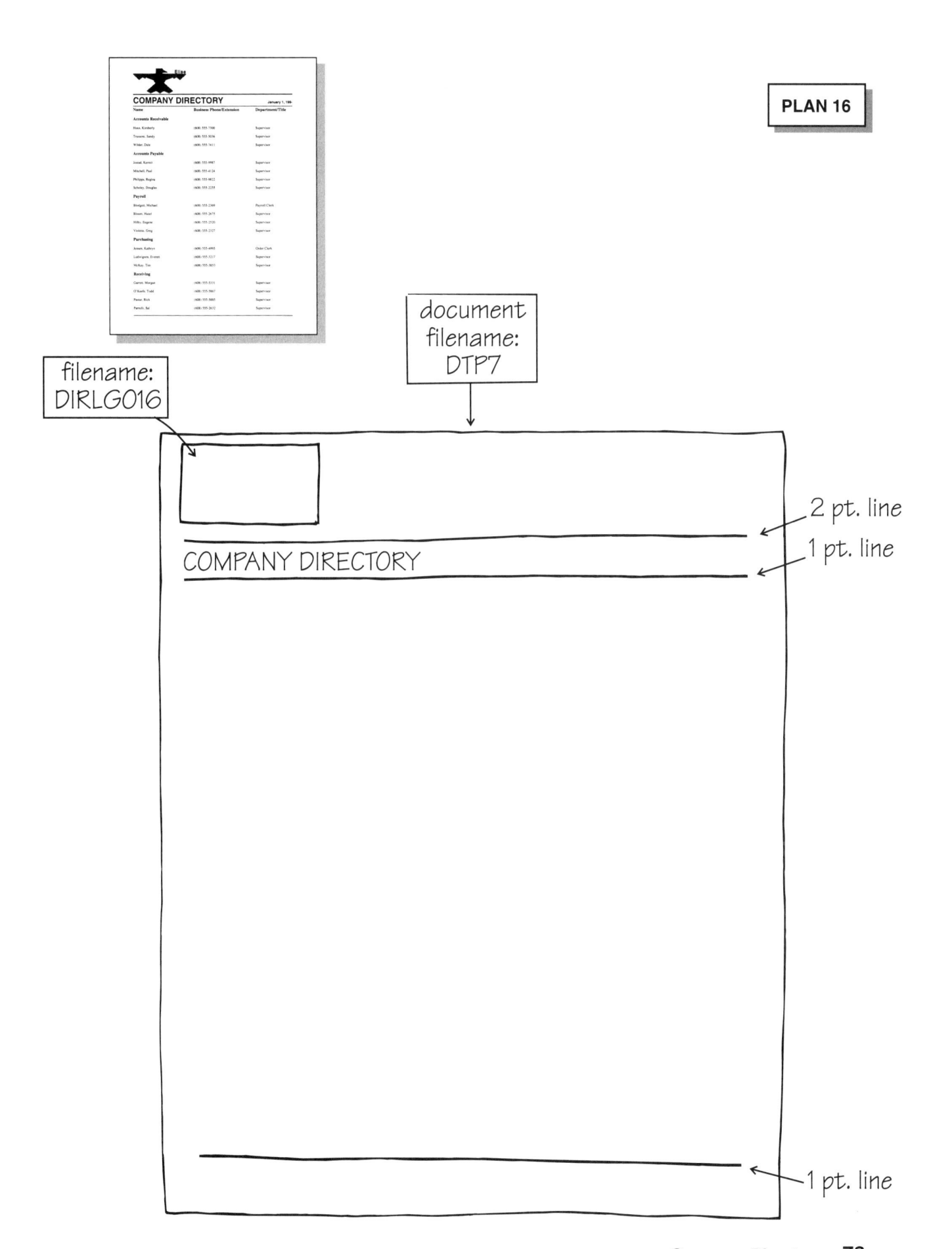

filename: DIRLGO16

document filename: DTP7

COMPANY DIRECTORY

2 pt. line
1 pt. line

1 pt. line

Name _____
Section _____ Date _____

Application 17 Product Specification Sheet with Graphics

Using the product specification sheet you began in application 8, add a vertical line between the columns along with a graphic to help guide the reader's eye to the important information.

1. Open file DTP8.
2. Create 2-point horizontal lines as indicated in plan 17.
3. Create the 4-point vertical line between the columns.

Hint Scaling is the process of increasing or decreasing the size of the graphic.

4. Import the graphic SPEC17G and place it above the third horizontal line in column 1. Scale the graphic to an appropriate size.
5. Save the publication as DTP17.
6. Proof your work. Make any changes or corrections. Save again if necessary.
7. Print DTP17.
8. Proof the printed document. Make corrections and print again if necessary.
9. Close the file.

Complete the entire exercise before answering the review questions.

Review

1. Are the horizontal rules of equal length?

   _____

2. To the nearest 1/100 of an inch, how thick is a 1-point line?

   _____

75

3. Which is thicker, a 1-point line or an 8-point line?

   _____

4. When scaling a graphic, what procedure do you follow to maintain the original proportions?

   _____

   _____

5. What is the difference between cropping and scaling a graphic?

   _____

   _____

6. Does the addition of graphics improve the quality of the document? Why or why not?

   _____

   _____

PLAN 17

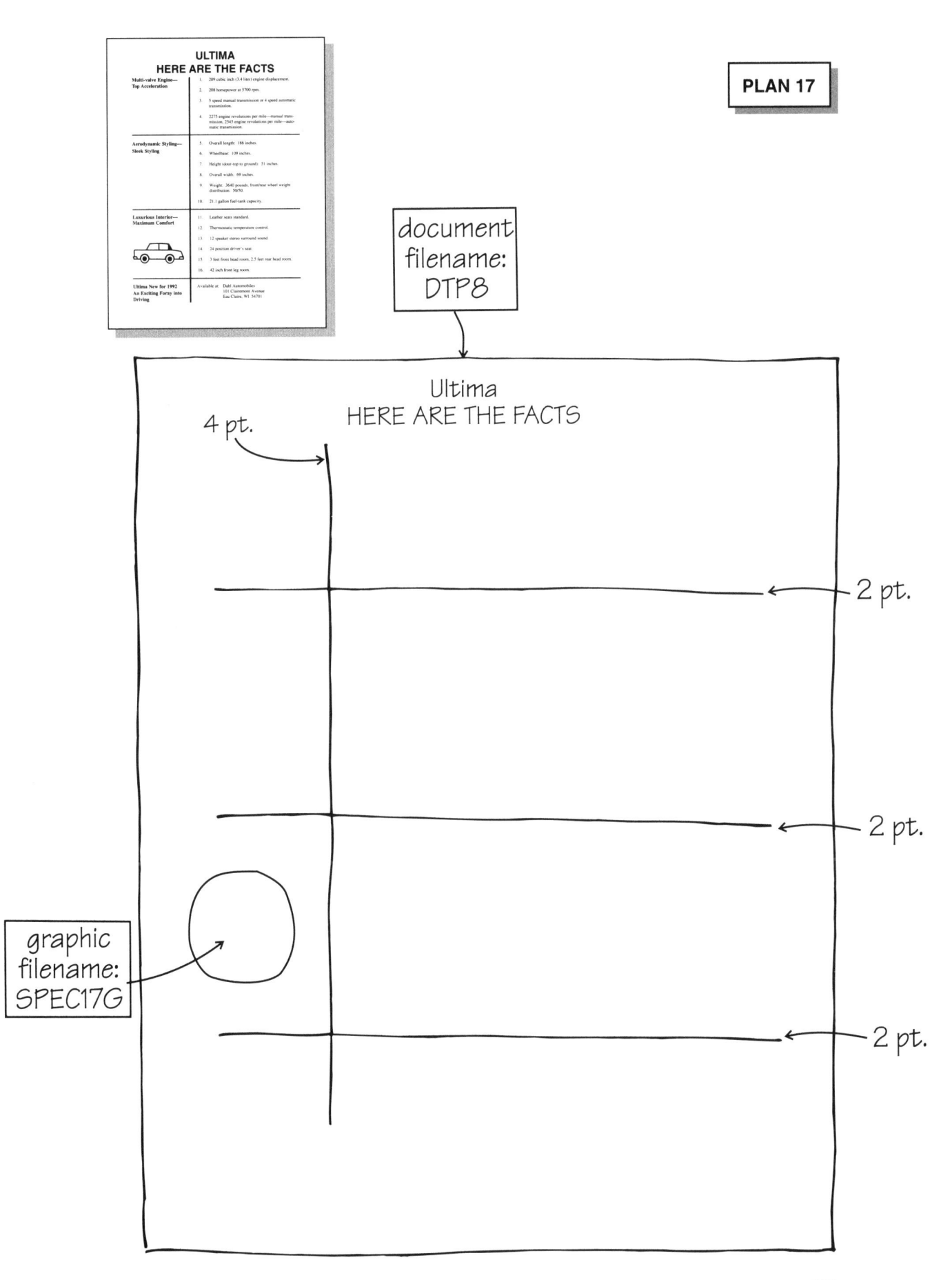

document filename: DTP8

Ultima
HERE ARE THE FACTS

4 pt.

2 pt.

2 pt.

graphic filename: SPEC17G

2 pt.

Name _____

Section _____ Date _____

Application 18 Enhanced Seminar Advertisement

Seminar advertisements need eye-catching appeal to be effective. Using the brochure you began in application 9, add boxes and graphics to enhance the document's appeal.

1. Open file DTP9.

Hint Lines, boxes, and shade patterns add visual interest to your document.

2. Import the graphic BACGR18 and place it according to plan 18. Scale the graphic to the correct size if necessary.
3. Replace each bullet on the back of the cover with an appropriately sized line and box. Create the line and box once. Copy and paste them to all locations necessary.
4. Add the box and shadow on the front cover.
5. Save the publication.
6. Proof your work. Make any changes or corrections. Save again if necessary.
7. Print DTP18.
8. Proof the printed document. Make corrections and print again if necessary.
9. Close the file.

Complete the entire exercise before answering the review questions.

Review

1. After folding the brochure, what are the measurements of all four margins?

   _____

   _____

2. Does the addition of graphics improve the quality of the document? Why or why not?

   _____

   _____

PLAN 18

graphic: BACGR18

add boxes and lines for each statement

document filename: DTP9

add box and shadow

landscape 11" x 8½"

80 • Seminar Advertisement

Name _____

Section _____ Date _____

Application 19 Public Relations Sheet with Illustration

Public relations materials can greatly benefit an organization. The wedding tips throw sheet you prepared in application 10 needs additional graphics for appeal. Adding an illustration depicting the information on the sheet, as well as rules to guide the eye, enhances this document.

1. Open DTP10.
2. Create a hairline above and between the two columns of text. Refer to plan 19.
3. Add 1-point lines at the top and bottom of the document.
4. Add the graphic GR19 in the lower right corner as shown in the plan. Scale if necessary.
5. Save the publication as DTP19.
6. Proof your work. Make any changes or corrections. Save again if necessary.
7. Print DTP19.
8. Proof the printed document. Make corrections and print again if necessary.
9. Close the file.

> Complete the entire exercise before answering the review questions.

Review

1. What part of the document offsets the graphic so the publication appears balanced?

   _____

   _____

2. Is the graphic balanced in white space?

   _____

3. What changes would you recommend to the client to improve this publication?

   _____

   _____

4. Would you change the title typeface to sans serif? Why?

   _____

   _____

   _____

5. Does the addition of graphics improve the quality of the document? Why or why not?

   _____

   _____

   _____

PLAN 19

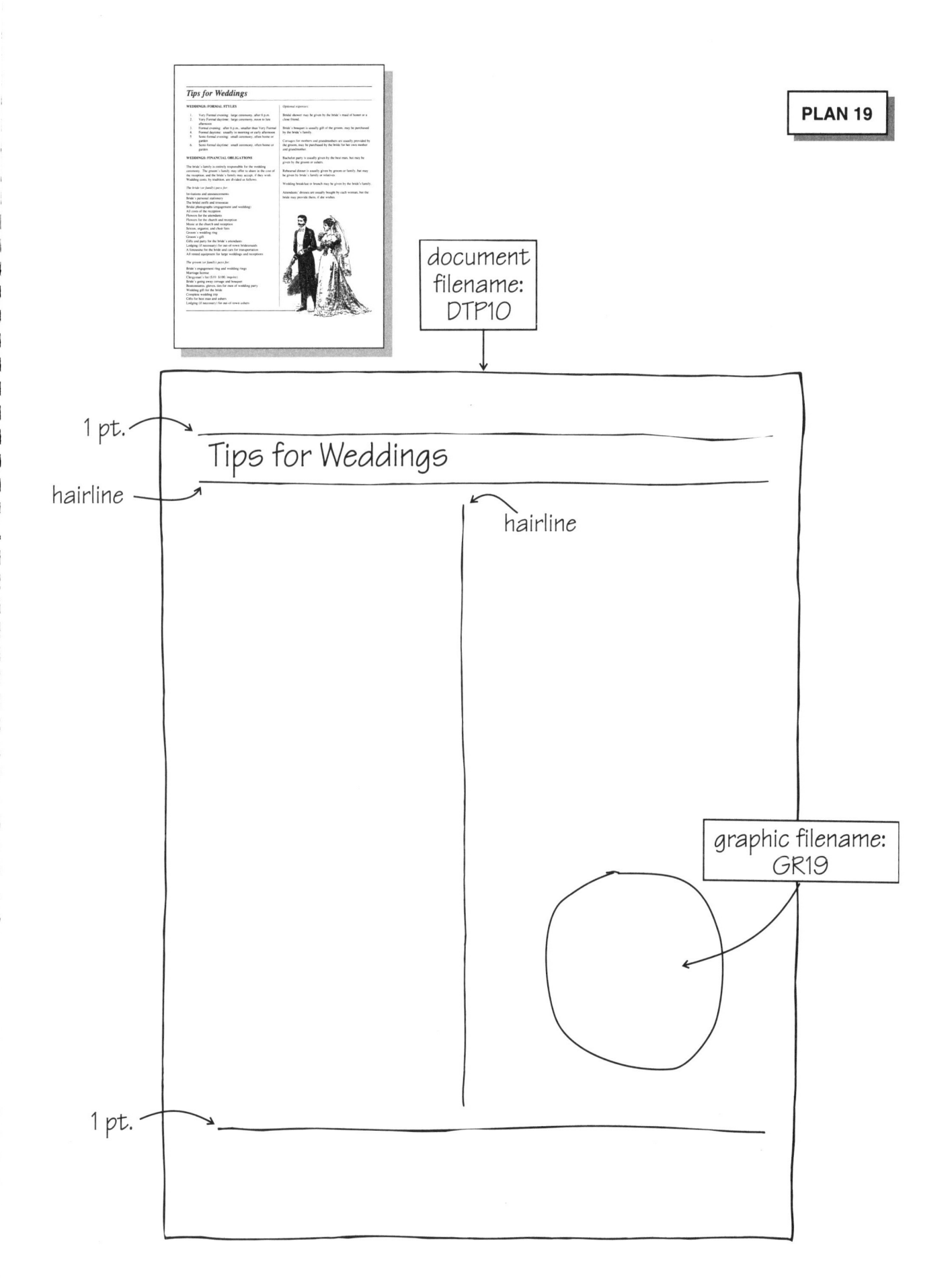

document filename: DTP10

Tips for Weddings

graphic filename: GR19

1 pt.

hairline

hairline

1 pt.

Name _____

Section _____ Date _____

Application 20 Poster with Boxes and Rules

Text alone can be enhanced by shading and by lines of different sizes. Using the document already produced in application 11, add basic gray boxes and rules to enhance the document.

1. Open DTP11.
2. Enclose the center pull-quote in a lightly shaded (10%) box.
3. Add the horizontal lines at the top and bottom as indicated in plan 20. Add the horizontal lines at the top and bottom of the shaded box. The lines at the top and bottom help balance the text and frame the screened pull-quote.
4. Add the lines above and below the nameplate.
5. Save the publication as DTP20.
6. Proof your work. Make any changes or corrections. Save again if necessary.
7. Print DTP20.
8. Proof the printed document. Make corrections and print again if necessary.
9. Close the file.

> Complete the entire exercise before answering the review questions.

Review

1. What is the procedure for moving an object to the front of a group of objects?

   _____

   _____

2. What is the procedure for moving an object to the back of a group of objects?

   _____

   _____

3. Does the addition of graphics improve the quality of the document? Why or why not?

   _____

   _____

PLAN 20

document filename: DTP11

R

this line thicker than this one

lightly shaded (10%)

T̲H̲E̲ H̲EALTH R̲EPORT

86 • Poster with Boxes and Rules

Name _____

Section _____ Date _____

Application 21 Recruitment Advertisement with Graphics

Your firm has been hired to create an eye-catching recruitment advertisement suitable for posting on a bulletin board. Using the document you created in application 12, enhance its readability with graphics.

1. Open DTP12.
2. Import the logo LOGO21 and place it below the 7.5-inch ruler guide as indicated in plan 21.
3. Add the first shaded box (20%), which is approximately .4 inch deep. Place it above the body text.
4. Make a copy of the shaded box you just created and place it below the body text.
5. Create a thin box around the entire advertisement .5 inch from the outer edge of the page.
6. Save the publication as DTP21.
7. Proof your work. Make any changes or corrections. Save again if necessary.
8. You may want to experiment with the leading of the body text to increase the readability and fill the available space.
9. Print DTP21.
10. Proof the printed document. Make corrections and print again if necessary.
11. Close the file.

> Complete the entire exercise before answering the review questions.

1. What is the procedure for duplicating a graphic?

   _____

   _____

2. Does the addition of graphics improve the quality of the document? Why or why not?

   _____

   _____

PLAN 21

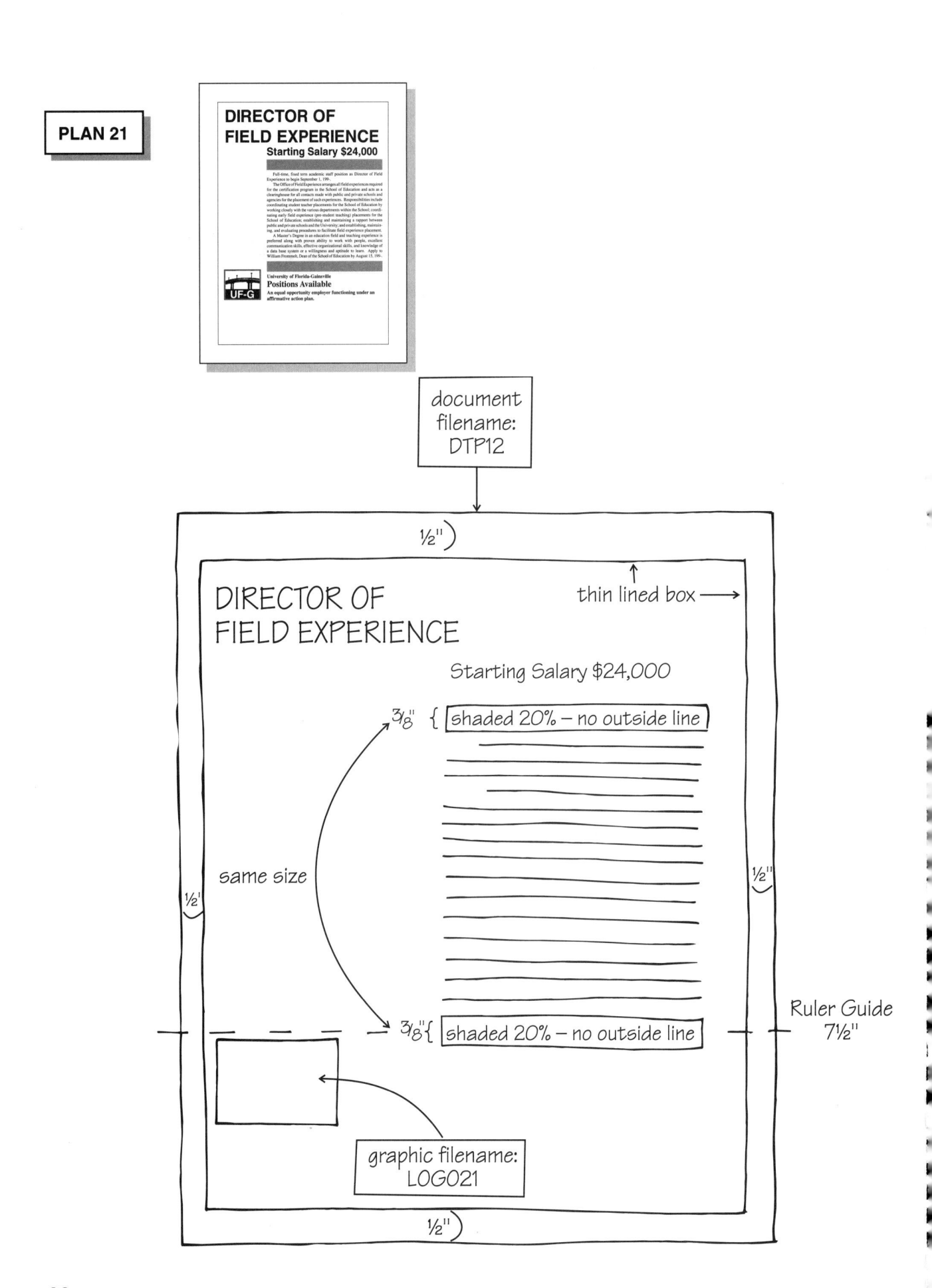

Sample advertisement:

DIRECTOR OF FIELD EXPERIENCE
Starting Salary $24,000

Full-time, fixed term academic staff position as Director of Field Experience to begin September 1, 199-.

The Office of Field Experience arranges all field experiences required for the certification program in the School of Education and acts as a clearinghouse for all contacts made with public and private schools and agencies for the placement of such experiences. Responsibilities include coordinating student teacher placements for the School of Education by working closely with the various departments within the School, coordinating early field experience (pre-student teaching) placements for the School of Education, establishing and maintaining a rapport between public and private schools and the University; and establishing, maintaining, and evaluating procedures to facilitate field experience placement.

A Master's Degree in an education field and teaching experience is preferred along with proven ability to work with people, excellent communication skills, effective organizational skills, and knowledge of a data base system or a willingness and aptitude to learn. Apply to William Frommelt, Dean of the School of Education by August 15, 199-.

University of Florida-Gainsville
UF-G
Positions Available

An equal opportunity employer functioning under an affirmative action plan.

---

document filename: DTP12

Layout sketch:

- ½" top margin
- thin lined box
- DIRECTOR OF FIELD EXPERIENCE
- Starting Salary $24,000
- ⅜" { shaded 20% – no outside line }
- same size
- ½" left margin
- ½" right margin
- ⅜" { shaded 20% – no outside line }
- Ruler Guide 7½"
- graphic filename: LOGO21
- ½" bottom margin

---

88 • **Recruitment Advertisement with Graphics**

Name _____
Section _____ Date _____

Application 22 Survey with Highlighting

Using the survey you began in application 13, add graphics by using the graphics tools available in your software. Be sure to use shading to highlight important information and to draw the reader's eye to items of importance.

1. Open DTP13.
2. Using your desktop graphics capabilities, create the check boxes in front of each topic if you have not already done so.
3. Add thin lines below **Name, Title, Company,** etc.
4. Add the horizontal lines as shown in plan 22.
5. Save the document as DTP22.
6. Add the thin lines in the **...And...** section.
7. Create a heavily shaded (40%) box and place it behind the text SRVEY13B. Reverse the lines in this area so that they are white on the background if possible.
8. Save the publication.
9. Proof your work. Make any changes or corrections. Save again if necessary.
10. Print DTP22.
11. Proof the printed document. Make corrections and print again if necessary.
12. Close the file.

Complete the entire exercise before answering the review questions.

Review

1. What is the process for reversing the lines so that they appear white on the gray background?

   _____
   _____

2. What is the process for moving text to the foreground?

   _____
   _____

3. Does the addition of graphics improve the quality of the document? Why or why not?

   _____
   _____

PLAN 22

document filename: DTP13

Would you read us?

(TEXT)

Planning

Promotion

Technologies

. . . And . . .

Name

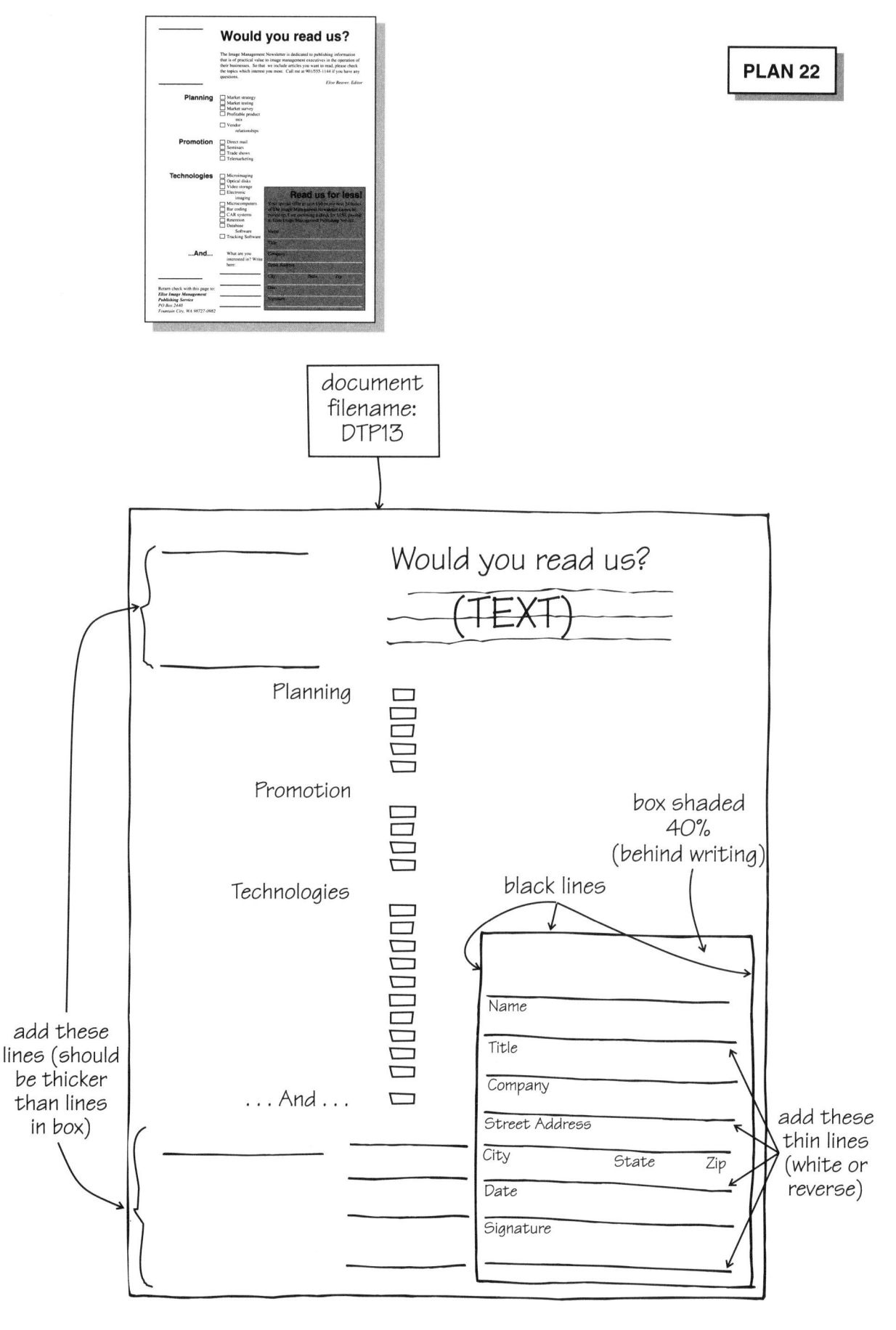

Title

Company

Street Address

City   State   Zip

Date

Signature

- box shaded 40% (behind writing)
- black lines
- add these lines (should be thicker than lines in box)
- add these thin lines (white or reverse)

Survey with Highlighting • 91

Name _____
Section _____ Date _____

Application 23 Enhanced Trifold Flyer

Graphics in trifold flyers help the reader identify the major information being presented. In the case of the information you created in Application 14, adding pictures of instruments is very appropriate. Stretch the graphics to fit the area. This stretch gives a professional appearance to an otherwise plain flyer.

1. Open DTP14.
2. Add the graphics INST1, INST2, and INST3, as indicated in plan 23. Elongate the graphics.
3. Save the document as DTP23.

Note When technology permits, a good attention-getting technique is to have a graphic *bleed* off the page. To bleed is to print a graphic to the edge of the page so there is no margin or white space.

4. Create the logo as shown in lower right corner of plan 23. If your printer allows, bleed this graphic off the bottom of the page.
5. Add the horizontal lines.
6. Save the publication.
7. Proof your work. Make any changes or corrections. Save again if necessary.
8. Print DTP23. Be sure to select auto tiling and crop marks to assemble the final product. (See application 14 for further explanation.)
9. Proof the printed document. Make corrections and print again if necessary.
10. Close the file.

Complete the entire exercise before answering the review questions.

Review

1. What is the procedure for distorting a graphic?
   _____
   _____

2. Does the addition of graphics improve the quality of the document? Why or why not?
   _____
   _____

PLAN 23

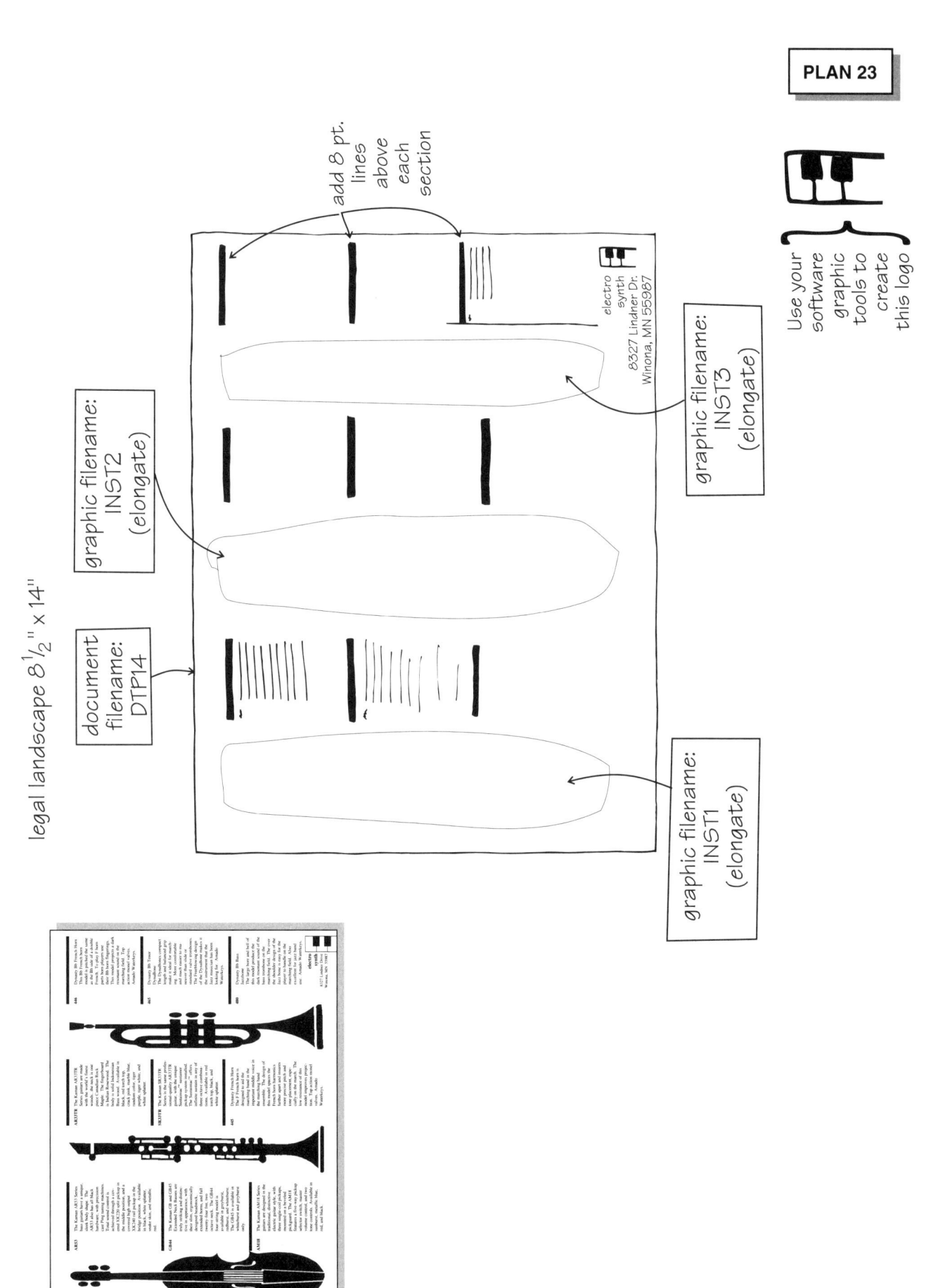

legal landscape 8½" x 14"

add 8 pt. lines above each section

graphic filename: INST2 (elongate)

document filename: DTP14

graphic filename: INST3 (elongate)

graphic filename: INST1 (elongate)

electro synth
8327 Lindner Dr.
Winona, MN 55987

Use your software graphic tools to create this logo

Enhanced Trifold Flyer • 95

Name _____
Section _____ Date _____

Application 24 **Price List with Illustrations**

Once again, you will add graphics to enhance the appearance of a document. This price list from application 15 needs graphics or pictures to help the reader easily identify what the content of the document presents.

1. Open DTP15.
2. Separate the sections with a thick line. Separate the subsections by a thinner line, shorter than the section line.
3. Save the document as DTP24.
4. Import the graphics PART1, PART2, PART3, PART4, PART5, PART6, PART7, and PART8. Place them at the 2-inch ruler guide. Scale appropriately. If your software permits, crop the graphic to eliminate any extra lines that were scanned. Refer to plan 24.
5. Save the document.
6. Import the company logo graphic LOGO24. Place it at the upper left corner. Scale the graphic to an appropriate size if necessary.
7. Save the publication.
8. Proof your work. Make any changes or corrections. Save again if necessary.
9. Print DTP24.
10. Proof the printed document. Make corrections and print again if necessary.
11. Close the file.

> Complete the entire exercise before answering the review questions.

Review

1. Because of the number and location of the graphics in this publication, it is very important to have them aligned appropriately. At what point on the horizontal ruler are the graphics aligned?

   _____

   _____

2. In this publication, you must proofread to ensure that the graphics are matched to the appropriate text. Do the pictures and the text match?

   _____

   _____

3. Does the addition of graphics improve the quality of the document? Why or why not?

   _____

   _____

PLAN 24

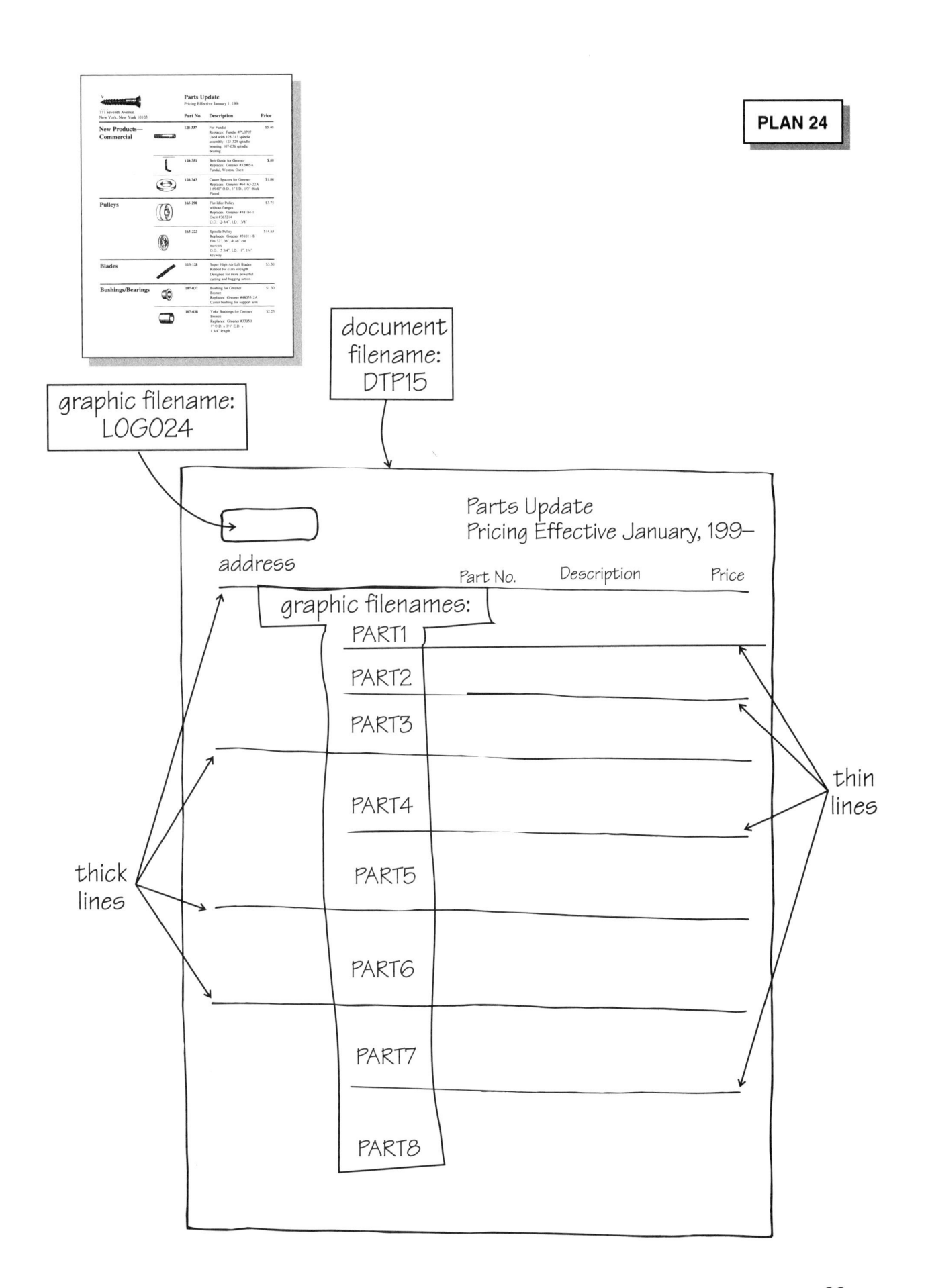

graphic filename: LOGO24

document filename: DTP15

Parts Update
Pricing Effective January, 199–

Part No.   Description   Price

address

graphic filenames:
PART1
PART2
PART3
PART4
PART5
PART6
PART7
PART8

thick lines

thin lines

Price List with Illustrations • 99

Name _____

Section _____ Date _____

Application 25 Floral Flyer

Your firm has been hired to create a one-page promotional piece for a large wholesale florist. The piece will be distributed to all customers as a service.

1. Create a new file.
2. Import the graphic for the flyer ROSE25.
3. Scale the graphic so that it fills approximately three-quarters of the area within the margins. Center the graphic on the page. See plan 25.
4. Import the body copy for the flyer PBS25. Place it below the top margin at the left margin.
5. Change the body copy to a serif, 12-point, bold, justified typeface. Do not indent paragraphs.
6. Key the heading using an appropriate font, style and size. Center the heading.
7. Change the leading and width of the text to center the text within the margins.
8. Save the document as DTP25.
9. Proof your work. Make any changes or corrections. Save again if necessary.
10. Print DTP25.
11. Proof the printed document. Make corrections and print again if necessary.
12. Close the file.

> Complete the entire exercise before answering the review questions.

Review

1. What is the procedure for changing the gray scale of an imported graphic image?

   _____

   _____

2. Looking at your printed publication, what conclusions can you draw about placing text over graphic images?

   _____

   _____

3. What is the procedure for getting text to wrap around a nonrectangular-shaped graphic?

   _____

   _____

4. Does the addition of graphics improve the quality of the document? Why or why not?

   _____

   _____

PLAN 25

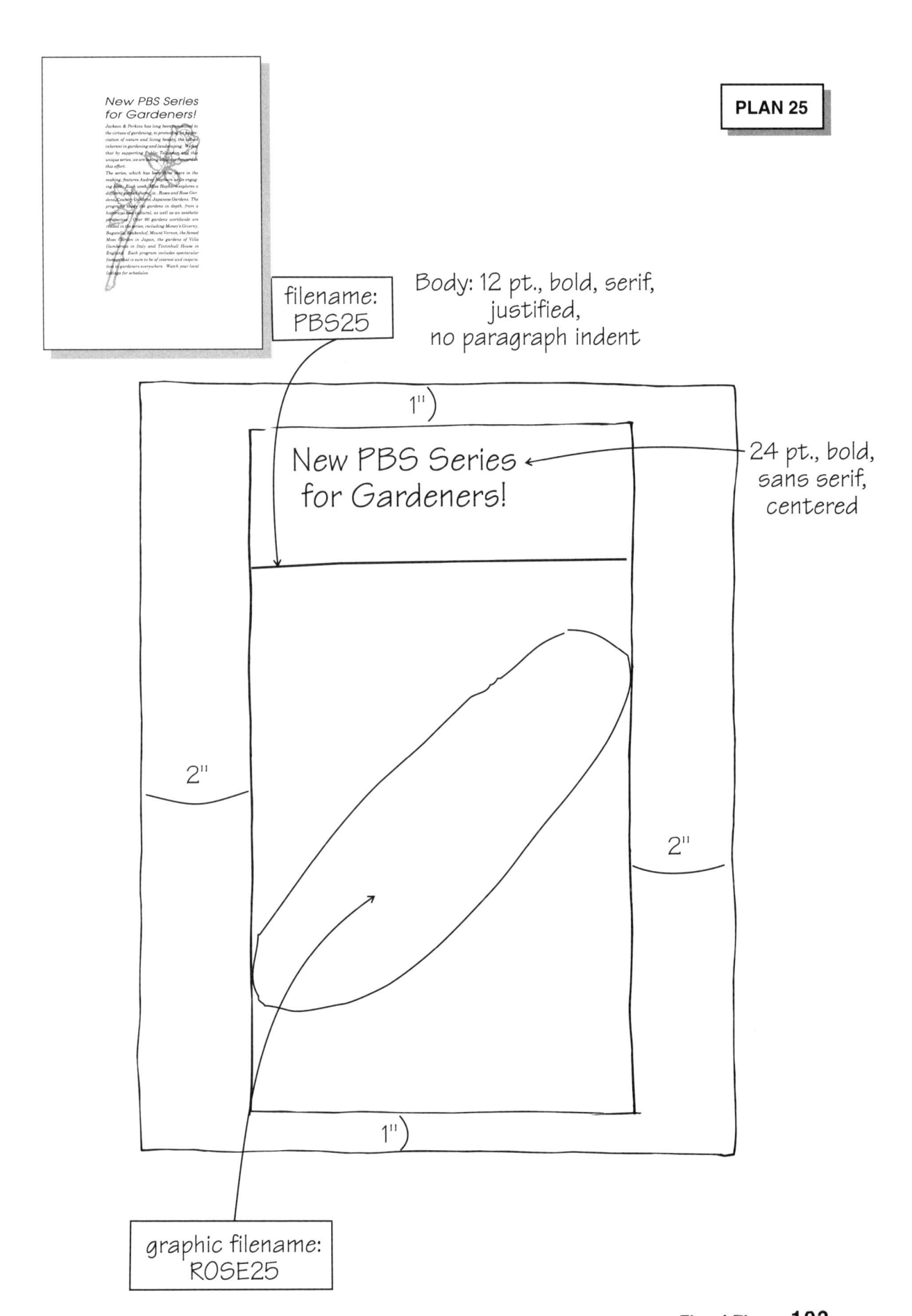

New PBS Series for Gardeners!

filename: PBS25

Body: 12 pt., bold, serif, justified, no paragraph indent

1"

New PBS Series for Gardeners!

24 pt., bold, sans serif, centered

2"

2"

1"

graphic filename: ROSE25

Floral Flyer • 103

Name _____

Section _____ Date _____

Application 26 Newsletter I

Many visuals are required in the field of real estate to be profitable. You have been asked to lay out a newsletter that contains text and graphics. The newsletter will be sent to prospective customers and former customers as a service. There will be additional pages to this newsletter, but you are only to prepare the first page for approval by the real estate agents in the office.

1. Create a new file.
2. Create horizontal ruler guides 2 inches, 2.25 inches, and 4 inches down from the top of the document if your software permits.
3. Create the masthead of the newsletter as shown in plan 26.
4. Import the graphic element HOUSE26 at the bottom of the newsletter. Create the horizontal lines at the bottom of the newsletter.
5. Import the graphic for the newsletter HOUSE26. Place it below the 4-inch horizontal ruler guide in column 2. Scale the graphic proportionately to fill the space allotted for it in the plan. Enclose this graphic in a thin-ruled box. Choose the option that makes text wrap around the graphic.
6. Save the document as DTP26TEM. This template will be used in another application later.
7. Automatically flow text from column to column if possible. Import the body copy for the page TEXT26-1. Place it below the 2.25-inch ruler guide at the left margin.
8. Change the body copy to a serif, 12-point, left-justified typeface. Indent paragraphs .25 inch. Use a style sheet if possible.
9. Change the heading to a sans serif, 18 to 24-point, bold typeface. Left justify the heading.
10. Save the document as DTP26.

11. Import the text that will appear beneath the picture, TEXT26-2. This text should span both columns 2 and 3. Insert a graphic element or symbol at the beginning of each point. Choose an appropriate format, size, and style of type.
12. Save the flyer.
13. Proof your work. Make any changes or corrections. Save again if necessary.
14. Print DTP26.
15. Proof the printed document. Make corrections and print again if necessary.
16. Close the file.

> Complete the entire exercise before answering the review questions.

Review

1. What is the procedure for instructing your software to wrap text around a rectangular graphic image?

2. What is the procedure for creating three columns of equal width?

3. What is the procedure for ensuring that the text at the top of all three columns begins at the same point on the vertical ruler?

4. Does the addition of graphics improve the quality of the document? Why or why not?

PLAN 26

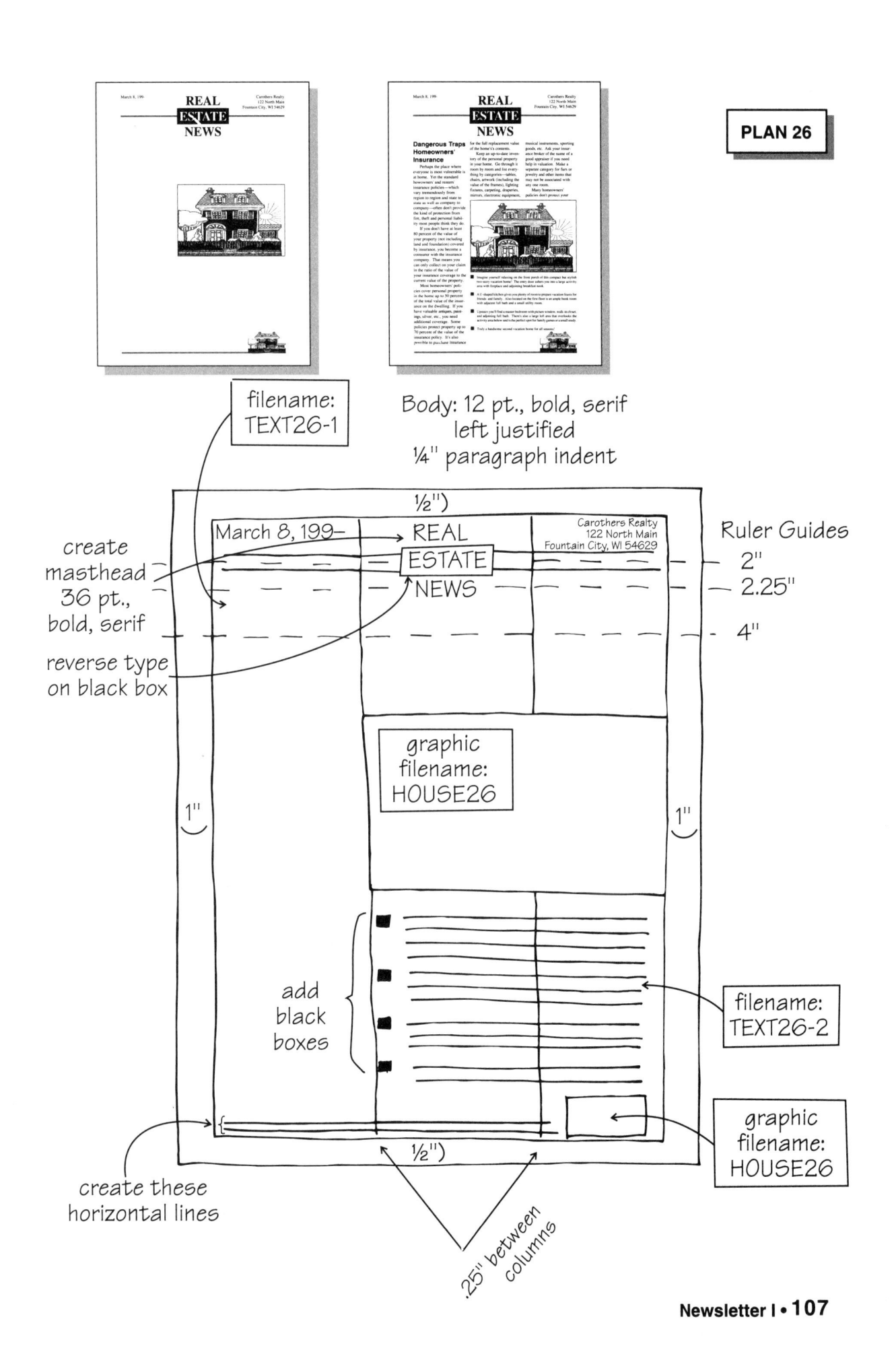

filename: TEXT26-1

Body: 12 pt., bold, serif
left justified
¼" paragraph indent

create masthead 36 pt., bold, serif

reverse type on black box

½")

March 8, 199–   REAL   Carothers Realty
                 ESTATE   122 North Main
                 NEWS   Fountain City, WI 54629

Ruler Guides
— 2"
— 2.25"
— 4"

1"   1"

graphic filename: HOUSE26

add black boxes

filename: TEXT26-2

graphic filename: HOUSE26

create these horizontal lines

½")

.25" between columns

Newsletter I • 107

Name _____

Section _____ Date _____

Application 27 Newsletter II

Your firm has been hired by a local business to develop its quarterly newsletter. This newsletter is the first page to be approved by the client before you continue with the rest of the document.

1. Create a new file. Refer to plan 27.

> **Hint** Standoff is the space between the outside edge of a graphic element and the text that surrounds the graphic.

2. Import the graphic GR27. Instruct your software to wrap the text around the graphic and to leave a .25-inch standoff at the top of the graphic.
3. Create a thin-ruled box around the graphic in columns 1 and 2.
4. Create the masthead information as two overlapping text blocks.

    LINK$_{AGE}$

    Add the rules in the masthead. Add the date.
5. Save the flyer as DTP27TEM for use later.
6. Create the title of the article according to the plan.

    THE LUTHERAN HOME—Cochrane...

    "The Mission Work Among the Handicapped Continues to Grow"
7. Import the text TEXT27A. Place the text according to figure 27.1.
8. Import the text TEXT27B. Place it according to plan 27.
9. Import the text TEXT27C. Place it according to plan 27.
10. Add the rules shown in the plan.
11. Save the document as DTP27.

109

12. Proof your work. Make any changes or corrections. Save again if necessary.

13. Print DTP27.

14. Proof the printed document. Make corrections and print and save again if necessary.

15. Close the file.

> Complete the entire exercise before answering the review questions.

Review

1. What procedure did you follow to change the boundary (offset) of the graphic?

   _____
   _____
   _____
   _____
   _____

2. Are the lines of text aligned horizontally from column to column? What procedure do you use to horizontally align columns of text?

   _____
   _____
   _____
   _____
   _____

PLAN 27

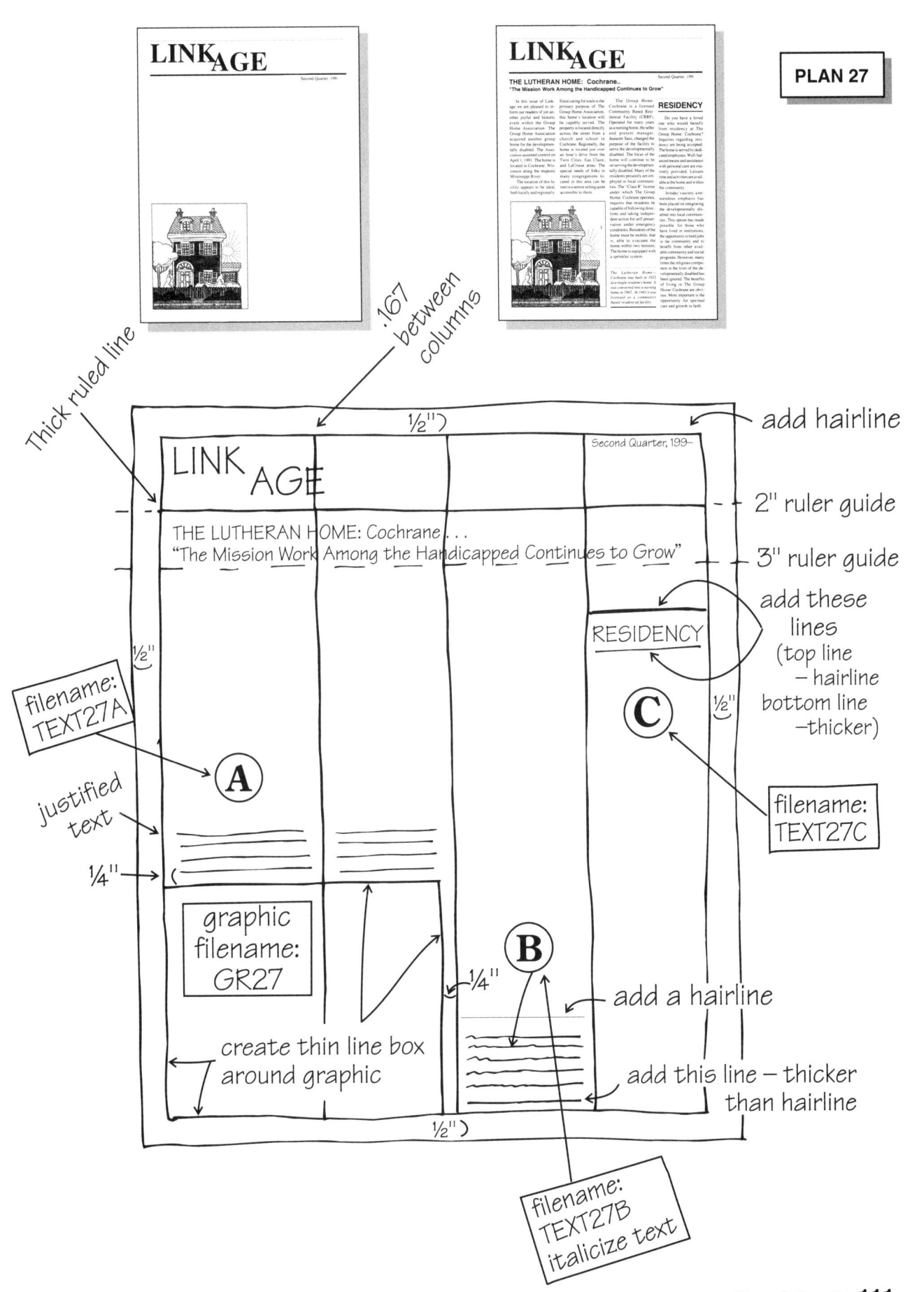

Thick ruled line

.167 between columns

½")

add hairline

LINK AGE

Second Quarter, 199–

2" ruler guide

THE LUTHERAN HOME: Cochrane...
"The Mission Work Among the Handicapped Continues to Grow"

3" ruler guide

½"

filename: TEXT27A

justified text

¼"

Ⓐ

RESIDENCY

add these lines
(top line
— hairline
bottom line
—thicker)

½"

Ⓒ

filename: TEXT27C

graphic filename: GR27

Ⓑ

¼"

add a hairline

create thin line box around graphic

add this line – thicker than hairline

½")

filename: TEXT27B
italicize text

Newsletter II • 111

Name _____

Section _____ Date _____

Application 28 Brochure I

You have been assigned the task of preparing a camera-ready brochure to market the health care educational outreach offerings. The finished publication is larger than 8.5" x 11" and requires you to stretch the capabilities of your standard laser printer. In doing so, you will have to prepare the document in sections so that you can prepare a master for duplication.

1. Create a new file. Notice the custom size indicated in plan 28.
2. Set all margins at .5 inch.
3. Create horizontal ruler guides 5.25, 5.75, 6, 11, and 14.5 inches from the top of the document if your software permits.
4. Create three columns. Their widths should be 2.75, 2.75, and 2.75 inches respectively.

   The gutters between the columns should be 3/8".

5. The space below the 5.75-inch ruler guide will be the front cover of this brochure. Type this information following the specifications in plan 28.

```
CONTINUING EDUCATION PROGRAMS
FOR
NURSES AND HEALTH CARE PROVIDERS
Rhinelander Community College
Rhinelander, New York
```

6. Create a graphic to surround the front cover similar to the one in plan 28 using the tools available in your desktop publishing package.
7. Save the flyer as DTP28.
8. Import the text CREDIT28, REFRSH28, LECT28, JRNAL28, and INDEP28. Place the text according to the plan. Use the hanging indent format for the enumerated items. The information in the last column should be set up using three tab sets. Format the text for ease of readability and so that all text fits in the space provided.
9. Save the flyer.

10. Create the shaded boxes as indicated in plan 28.
11. Import RETADD and MAILPER and place them according to the plan. If your software or printer is not able to rotate text, after printing you will cut and paste the return address and the mail permit so they are placed correctly when the brochure is folded.
12. Save.
13. Proof your work. Make any changes or corrections. Save again if necessary.

> **Hint** To print an oversized or enlarged publication in sections, or *tiles,* your page layout software has a tile or sections option in the print dialog or command box. This option divides your publication into sections that can be assembled for the final camera-ready product. Your software has the option of allowing the document to be sectioned or tiled automatically or manually. Crop marks will help you to align the sections. Cut the sections to align the overlapped tiles and then tape them using the crop marks for alignment.

14. When printing this large publication, choose tile and crop marks. Then cut and paste the tiles together for the camera-ready copy. Print DTP28.
15. Proof the printed document. Make corrections and print again if necessary.
16. Close the file.

> Complete the entire exercise before answering the review questions.

Review

1. What graphic tools does your desktop publishing software have?

   _____

   _____

2. Does the addition of graphics improve the quality of the document? Why or why not?

   _____

   _____

3. What is the purpose of tiling a document? When would this process be used?

   _____

   _____

PLAN 28

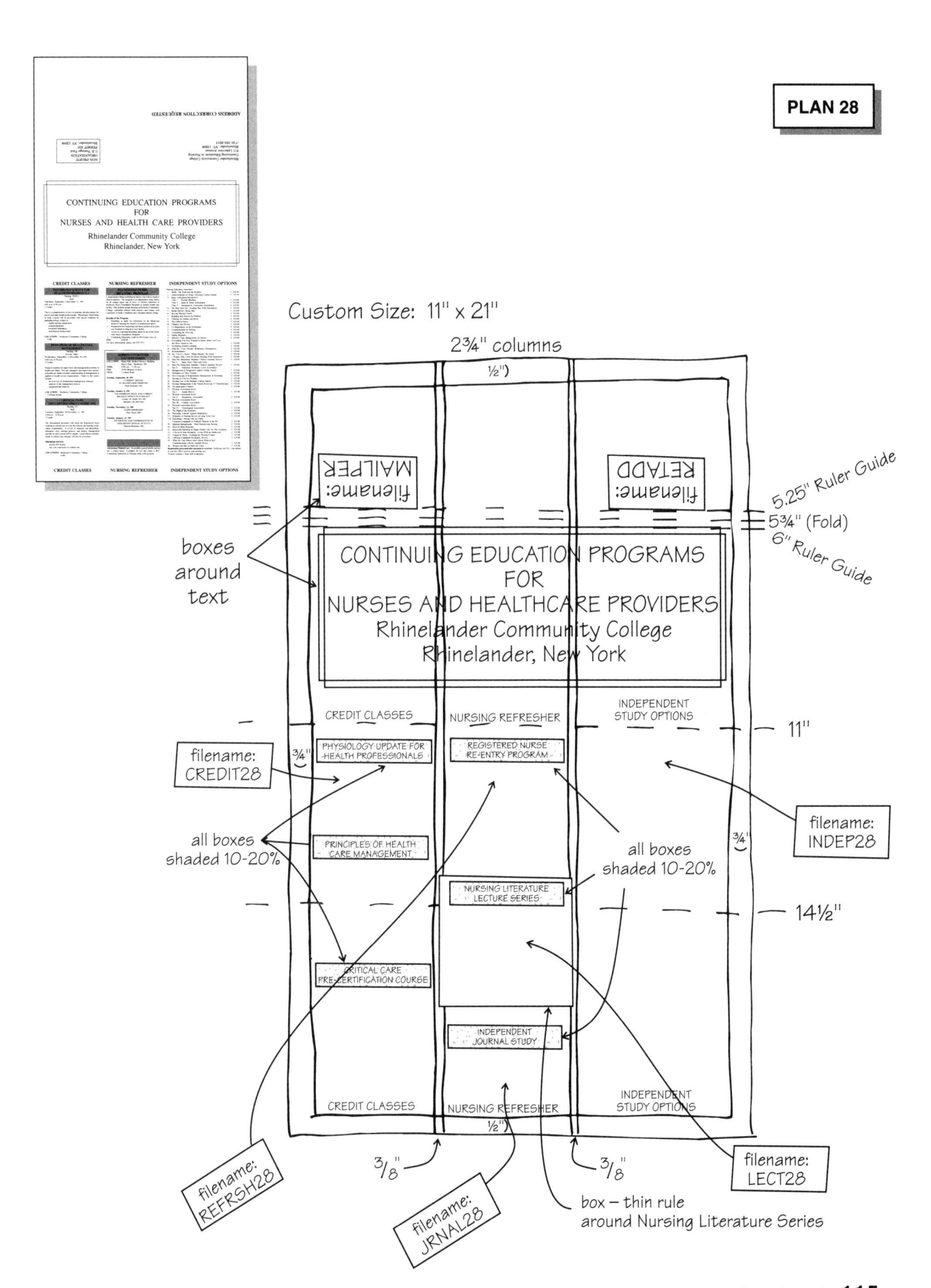

Custom Size: 11" x 21"

2¾" columns
(½")

**CONTINUING EDUCATION PROGRAMS
FOR
NURSES AND HEALTHCARE PROVIDERS
Rhinelander Community College
Rhinelander, New York**

filename: MAILPER
filename: RETADD

5.25" Ruler Guide
5¾" (Fold)
6" Ruler Guide

boxes around text

CREDIT CLASSES — NURSING REFRESHER — INDEPENDENT STUDY OPTIONS

11"

¾"

PHYSIOLOGY UPDATE FOR HEALTH PROFESSIONALS

REGISTERED NURSE RE-ENTRY PROGRAM

filename: CREDIT28

filename: INDEP28

all boxes shaded 10-20%

PRINCIPLES OF HEALTH CARE MANAGEMENT

all boxes shaded 10-20%

¾"

NURSING LITERATURE LECTURE SERIES

14½"

CRITICAL CARE PRE-CERTIFICATION COURSE

INDEPENDENT JOURNAL STUDY

filename: LECT28

CREDIT CLASSES — NURSING REFRESHER — INDEPENDENT STUDY OPTIONS
(½")

filename: REFRSH28

⅜"

filename: JRNAL28

⅜"

box – thin rule around Nursing Literature Series

Brochure I • 115

Name _____
Section _____ Date _____

Application 29 One-page Resume

Create a short one-page resume for a client. You may change the design or follow the plan given in plan 29.

1. Create a new file.
2. Use the file RESUME29 to create a resume similar to plan 29.

   Use the tab and indent options to arrange the text. Add the two rules with your graphic tools.
3. Save the resume as DTP29.
4. Proof your work. Make any changes or corrections. Save again if necessary.
5. Print DTP29.
6. Proof the printed document. Make corrections and print again if necessary.
7. Close the file.

> Complete the entire exercise before answering the review questions.

Review

1. Would additional rules enhance the aesthetic quality of the message? Why or why not?

   _____
   _____
   _____
   _____
   _____

PLAN 29

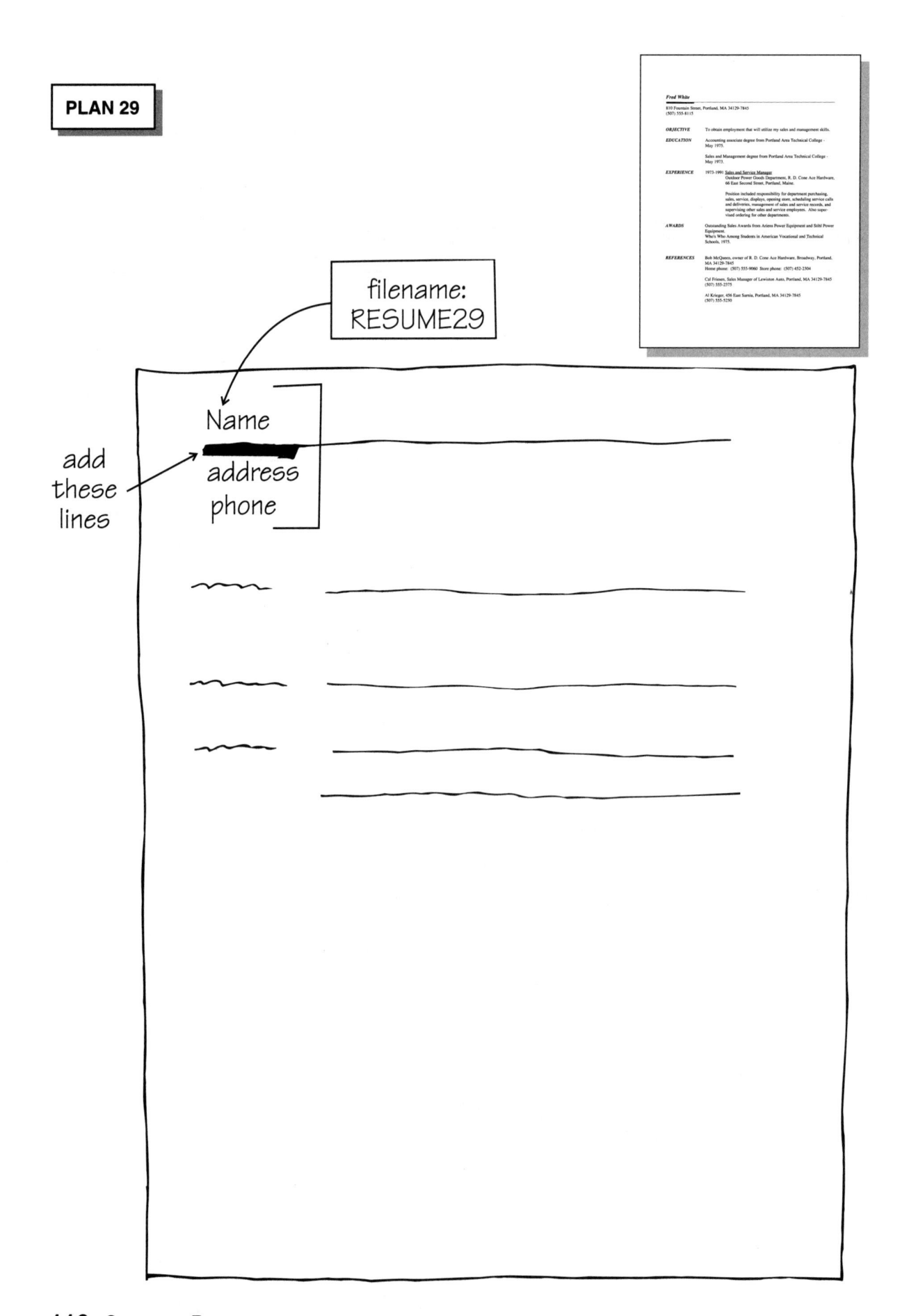

filename: RESUME29

add these lines → Name / address / phone

118 • **One-page Resume**

Name _____

Section _____ Date _____

Application 30 Brochure II

Create a brochure for a state professional organization. This brochure will be printed with light blue spot color.

Special copy preparation and pasteup techniques are required for color. The most common color designs are for two- and four-color reproduction.

Two-color design generally is used to focus attention on text to add visual interest. For example, a common practice is to print headings, key words, or other text elements in a color other than black. Used in this way, color helps to focus reader attention. Also, some elements of copy can be enclosed in color boxes, or screen tint blocks can be used as background. These techniques also help to emphasize text or illustrations. In addition, portions of line illustrations may be reproduced in color.

In printing, each color of ink is applied from a different plate. This means that separate platemaking film and printing plates must be prepared for each color on every color page.

With electronic desktop publishing, a separate output page is generated for each specified color. Each of the color pages contains registration marks and a code identifying the color. A registration mark is a symbol used to match the impressions of multiple colors. Registration marks are used to produce film and plates for printing.

Excessive use of color can do more harm than good, detracting from the message you are trying to convey. Keep in mind that it is best to use solid, dark colors for type. Light or pastel shades can be hard to read. Warm colors (reds, yellows, oranges) tend to be more exciting, while cool colors (blues, greens, violets) tend to be more calming. Warm colors are usually better used as accents, sparingly, whereas cool colors can be used more freely.

Color printing is more expensive than black-and-white printing. The more colors you use, the more costly it will be to print.

1. Create a new file using the specifications in plan 30.
2. Use the files ETHICS30, INTRNT30, TORT30, COMMUN30, and TELCOM30 to create the brochure.
3. Save the brochure as DTP30.
4. Create the graphics using the tools available in your software. These graphics will be printed using spot color.
5. The text that will be overlaid on the graphic in column 1 is, **Don't miss the opening session with Christy Varner, who presents her gripping true-life story as a highjacking victim.** The text for column 4 is, **'Humor is, ... No Laughing Matter!' is the topic of Michael Bohlinger's second general session.**
6. Change the paragraph spacing to .1 inch before the paragraph in the body text.
7. If your software permits, indicate that the graphics in columns 1 and 4 and the graphic at the top of the page should be printed in light blue spot color.
8. Save the brochure.
9. Proof your work. Make any changes or corrections. Save again if necessary.
10. Print DTP30. Remember to indicate that your printouts will be used to produce a publication with spot color.
11. Proof the printed document. Make corrections and print again if necessary.
12. Close the file.
13. Fold the publication along the 7-inch ruler guide.

Complete the entire exercise before answering the review questions.

Review

1. What are the procedures for indicating spot color in a publication?

_____
_____
_____

2. When and why would you use spot color in a publication?

   _____
   _____
   _____

3. What is the purpose of the paragraph spacing ability of your software?

   _____
   _____
   _____

4. If your software does not have the paragraph spacing capability, how might you compensate?

   _____
   _____
   _____

PLAN 30

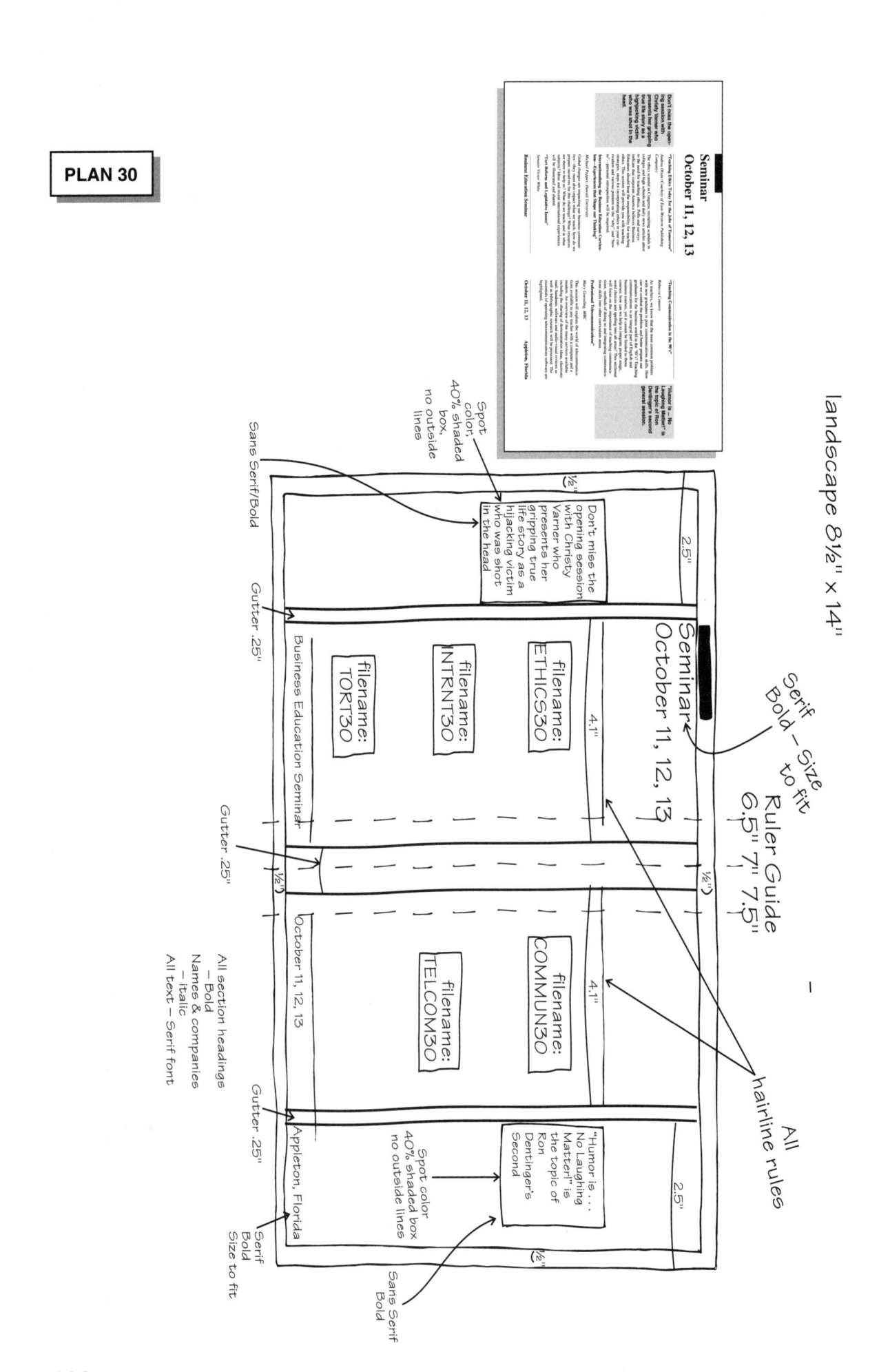

landscape 8½" × 14"

- Sans Serif/Bold
- Spot color, 40% shaded box, no outside lines
- Serif – Size to fit
- Ruler Guide 6.5", 7", 7.5"
- All hairline rules
- Gutter .25"
- Gutter .25"
- Gutter .25"
- Serif Bold Size to fit
- Sans Serif Bold

Boxes (left panel to right panel):
- "Don't miss the opening session with Christy Varner who presents her gripping true life story as a hijacking victim who was shot in the head." (2.5")
- filename: TORT30
- filename: INTRNT30
- filename: ETHICS30 (4.1")
- Seminar / October 11, 12, 13
- Business Education Seminar
- (½")
- (½")
- filename: COMMUN30
- filename: TELCOM30 (4.1")
- October 11, 12, 13
- Appleton, Florida
- "Humor is . . . No Laughing Matter!" is the topic of Ron Dentinger's Second (2.5")
- Spot color 40% shaded box no outside lines

All section headings
 — Bold
Names & companies
 — Italic
All text — Serif font

122 • Brochure II

Name _____
Section _____ Date _____

Application 31 Organizational Chart

Create the organizational chart as shown in plan 31 for a customer.

1. Create a new file. The dimensions of the publication are 8.5 inches x 11 inches. Choose tall as the orientation.

2. Use the file NAMES31 and your graphics tools to create an organizational chart similar to plan 31. Decide on the hierarchy from the titles. Lay out the chart in a more conventional manner, if you choose.

3. Save the file as DTP31.

4. Proof your work. Make any changes or corrections. Save again if necessary.

5. Print DTP31.

6. Proof the printed document. Make corrections and print again if necessary.

7. Close the file.

Complete the entire exercise before answering the review questions.

Review

1. Would it be more efficient to use the text already created and stored in NAMES31 or to rekey the text as needed? Why?

   _____
   _____
   _____
   _____

123

PLAN 31

filename: NAMES31

all titles bold, all text with a slant (italics) font

Kramer & Adams, Inc. Org. Chart — Bold

Kramer & Adams, Inc. — Bold
Westend Plaza
17289 Sarinia Street
Winona, Maine 65987

Unit 3
Performance Challenge

1. Open UNIT2PC.
2. Create the lines between the sections and the lines between the items. Section lines should be heavier than item lines. Refer to plan U3.
3. Remove the word **Warehouse** at the top of column 1.
4. Add the graphics at the top and bottom. Both graphics are part of the file PC3GR. Crop the graphic to retain only the portion you need for each graphic element.
5. Proof the document. Spell check the document if possible.
6. Save the file as UNIT3PC.
7. Print UNIT3PC.
8. Proof the document. Make any necessary corrections or adjustments.
9. Save the file.
10. Print again if necessary.

PLAN U3

add graphic and crop

graphic filename: PC3GR

Black or solid fill, reverse type

add graphic and crop

PRICE LIST

¾"

CW PRICE LIST

| Description | Price | Order # | PG. |

Labels

Basics

Filters

Disk Files

¾" ¾"

Covers

CFY   address

¾"

Unit 3 Performance Challenge • 127

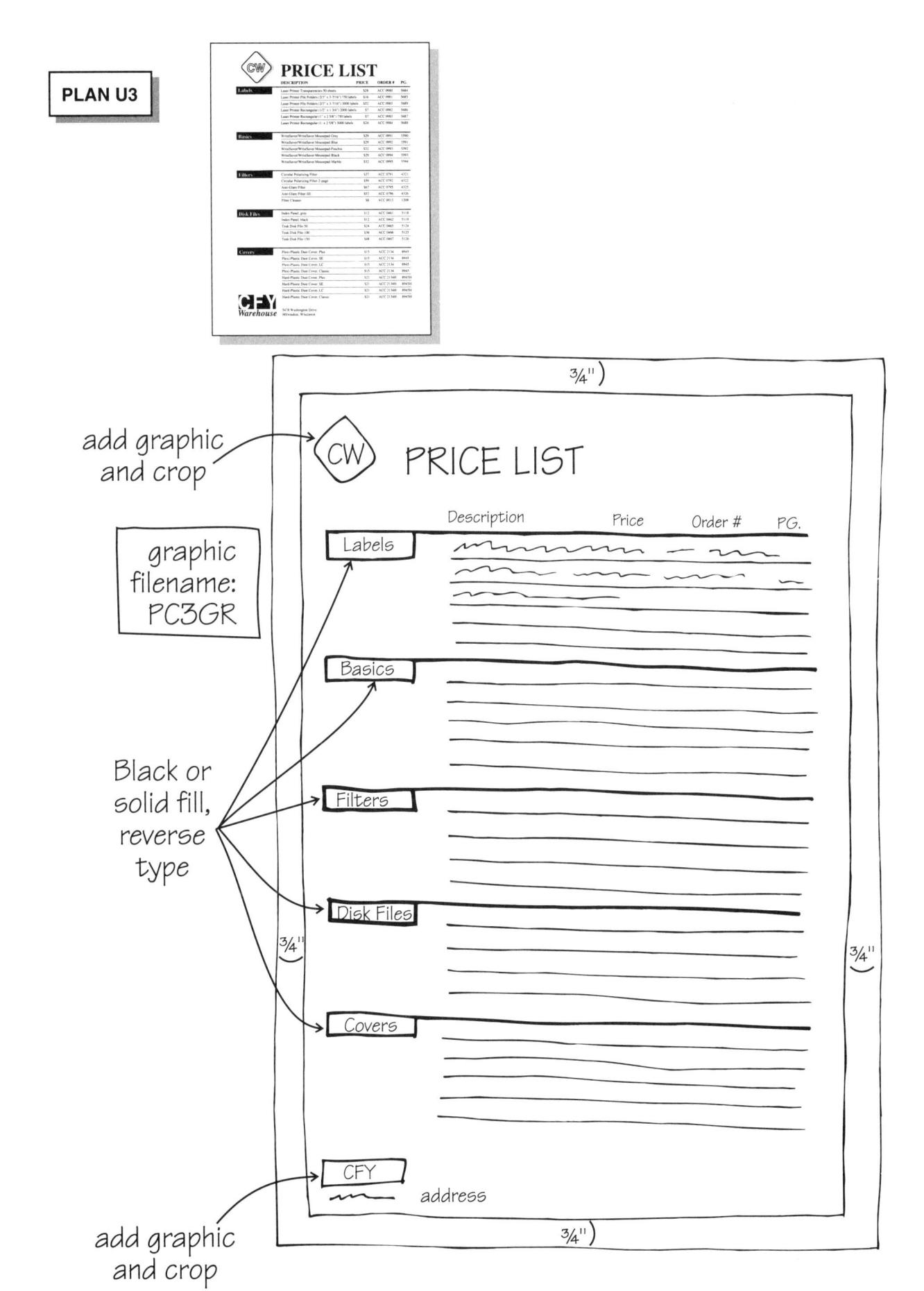

Unit 4
Designing Multipage Documents

The applications in this unit allow you to create multi-page documents. You will use the master pages, table of contents, and page number marker features of your software.

Finished documents will include two newsletters and several pages to be included in a booklet.

Before beginning the production of the publications in Unit 4, background information is needed. A master page is a nonprinting page that may contain ruler guides, column guides, text blocks, and graphics that are automatically displayed on all pages of the publication. For example, if you want a footer to appear on every page of the document, you would type that footer on the master page.

Name _____
Section _____ Date _____

Application 32 Newsletter I – Next Issue

Each month your firm creates a newsletter called Real Estate News for a client. In the past, a template containing the basic layout was saved as DTP26TEM. You will add current articles to this basic layout for the April issue.

1. Open DTP26TEM. Add/insert a page to the document to make it two pages.
2. Create the following master items:
    a. three columns of equal width on all pages;
    b. two horizontal rules at the bottom margin of all pages as shown in plan 32.
3. You may have to remove rules previously drawn on pages other than the master pages to avoid conflicts.
4. Save the template as DTP32TEM.
5. On page 1, change the date of the newsletter to April 9, 199–.
6. Import the articles as shown in plan 32. Adjust text boxes to fit text. (COLORGRD, ENERGY, WALKING.)
7. Replace the existing graphic in columns 2 and 3 with HOUSE2.
8. Proof the document. Spell check the document if possible.
9. Save the file as DTP32.
10. Print DTP32.
11. Proof the document. Make any necessary corrections or adjustments.
12. Save the file.
13. Print again if necessary.

> Complete the entire exercise before answering the review questions.

Review

1. How much time would you estimate you saved by using the template to begin this application? Will the time savings be greater the next time you use DTPTEM26? Why?

   _____
   _____
   _____
   _____
   _____

2. What is the procedure for replacing an existing graphic with a new graphic?

   _____
   _____
   _____
   _____

PLAN 32

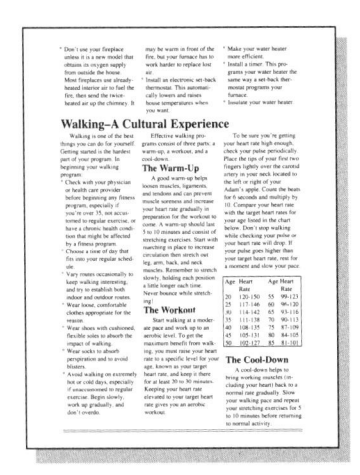

document filename: DTP26TEM

Body: 12 pt., serif
left justified
¼" paragraph indent

Article Headlines (found in text files)
24 pt., bold, serif
left justified

April 9, 199-

REAL ESTATE NEWS

filename: ENERGY

graphic filename: HOUSE2

filename: COLORGRD

page 1

graphic filename: HOUSE2

Bulleted items:
Set negative indent for .125"

ENERGY continued from pg. 1

Walking--A Cultural Experience

filename: WALKING

The Warm-Up

The Workout

The Cool-Down

page 2

Span head across all 3 columns
24 pt., bold, serif

Set tabs in heart rate table. Enclose table in box.

Subheads:
18 pt., bold, serif

Newsletter I — Next Issue • 133

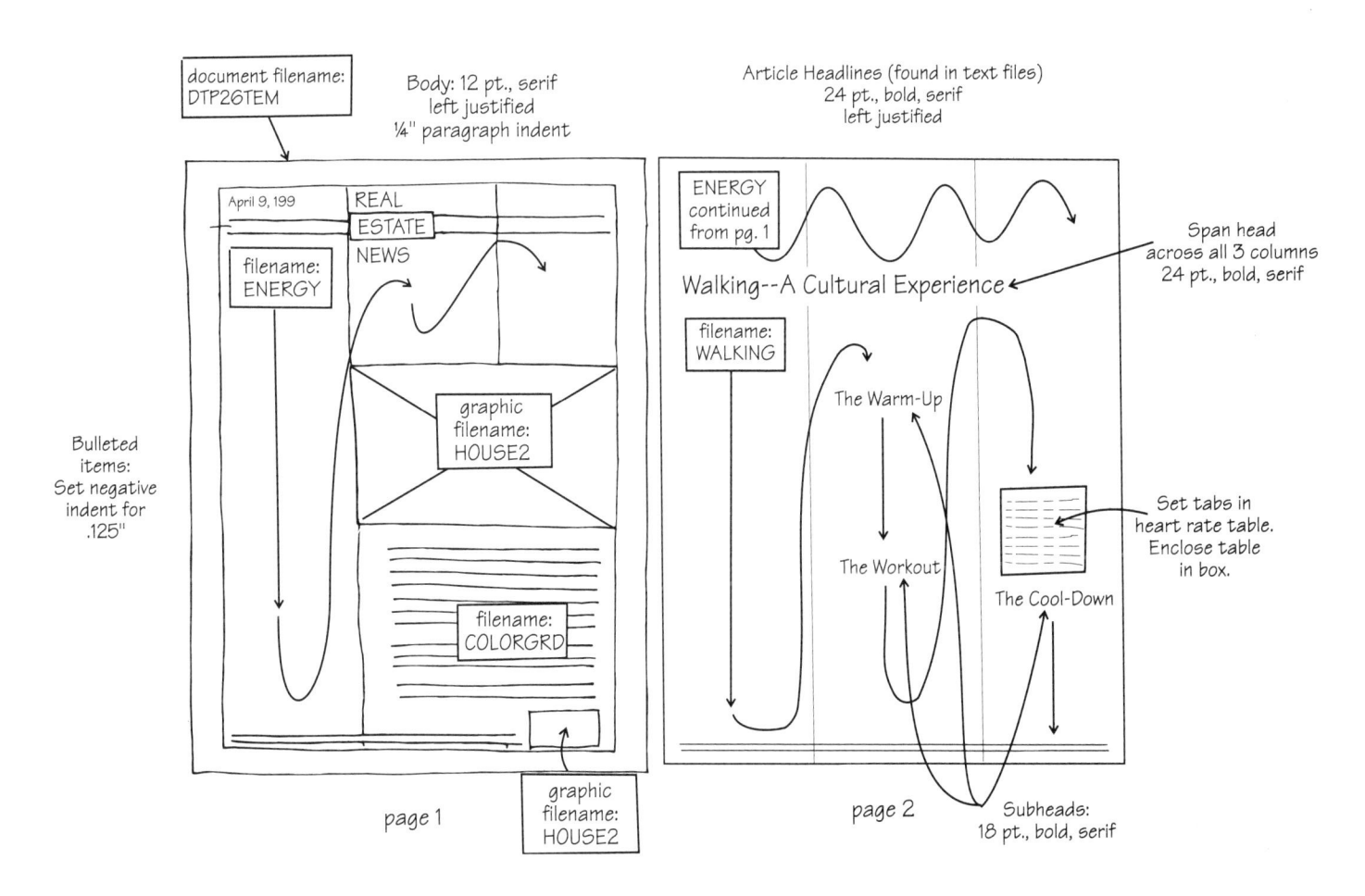

Name _____
Section _____ Date _____

Application 33 Newsletter II — Next Issue

Each month your firm creates a newsletter called Linkage for a client. In the past, a template containing basic layout was saved as DTP27TEM. You will add current articles to this basic layout for the third quarter issue.

1. Open DTP27TEM.
2. Create the following master items:
   a. four columns of equal width on all pages;
   b. a page number marker, **Linkage/Third Quarter** *Page 0*, at the bottom of the page(s).
3. Save the template as DTP33TEM.
4. On page 1, change the date of the newsletter to **Third Quarter, 199–**.
5. Import the articles as shown in plan 33. Size to fit.
6. Proof the document. Spell check the document if possible.
7. Save the file as DTP33.
8. Print DTP33.
9. Proof the document. Make any necessary corrections or adjustments.
10. Save the file.
11. Print again if necessary.

> Complete the entire exercise before answering the review questions.

Review

1. What is the procedure for creating a page number marker?
   _____
   _____

PLAN 33

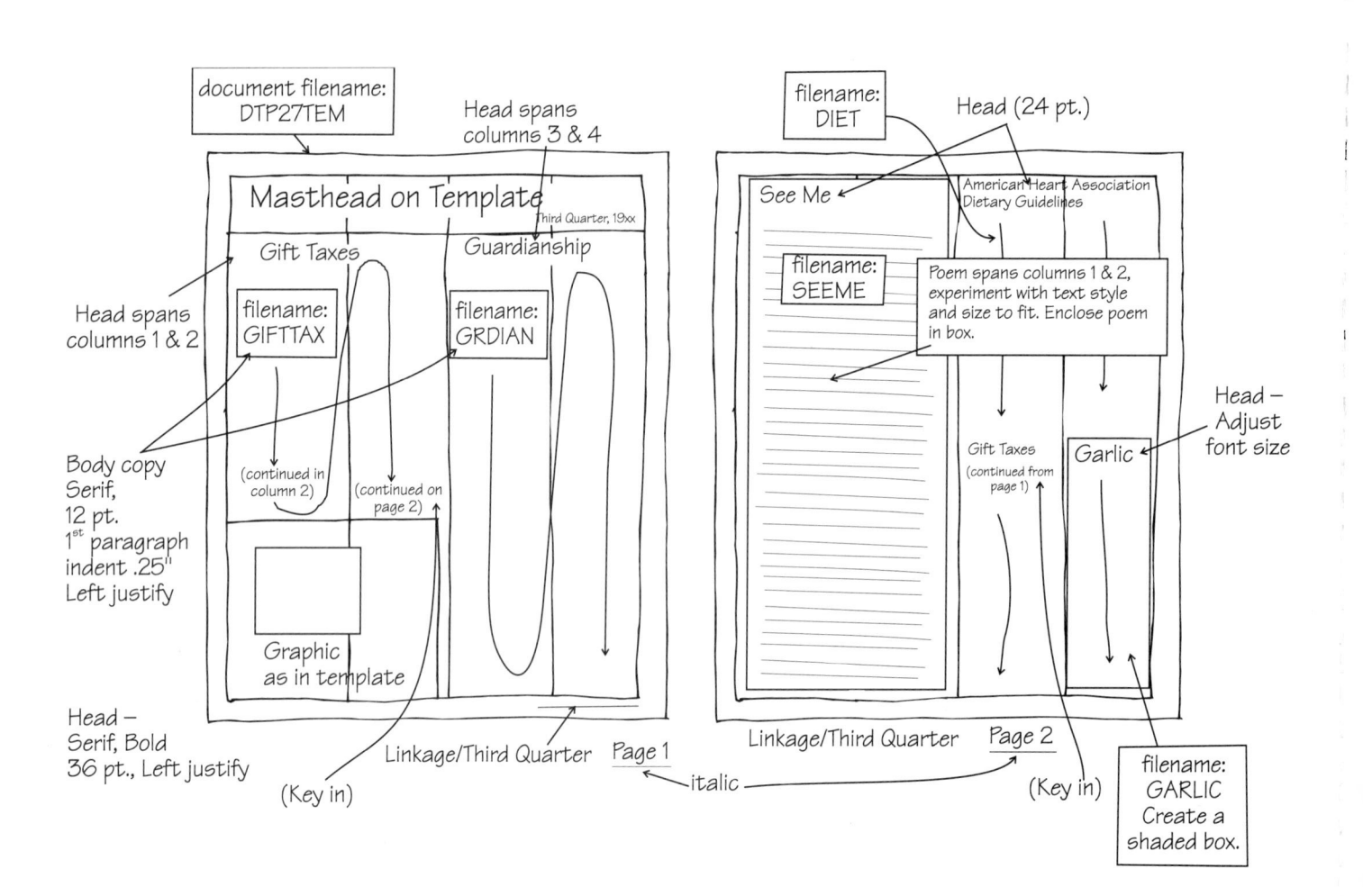

Page 1 mockup

LINKAGE

Third Quarter, 199-

Gift Taxes

Guardianship

Page 2 mockup

See Me

American Heart Association Dietary Guidelines

GARLIC

Page 1 layout notes

- document filename: DTP27TEM
- Masthead on Template
- Third Quarter, 19xx
- Head spans columns 3 & 4
- Gift Taxes — Head spans columns 1 & 2
- Guardianship
- filename: GIFTTAX
- filename: GRDIAN
- (continued in column 2)
- (continued on page 2)
- Graphic as in template
- Body copy Serif, 12 pt. 1st paragraph indent .25" Left justify
- Head – Serif, Bold 36 pt., Left justify
- Linkage/Third Quarter — italic
- Page 1 (Key in)

Page 2 layout notes

- filename: DIET
- Head (24 pt.)
- See Me
- American Heart Association Dietary Guidelines
- filename: SEEME
- Poem spans columns 1 & 2, experiment with text style and size to fit. Enclose poem in box.
- Gift Taxes (continued from page 1)
- Garlic
- Head – Adjust font size
- Linkage/Third Quarter
- Page 2 (Key in)
- filename: GARLIC Create a shaded box.

136 • Newsletter II — Next Issue

Unit 4
Performance Challenge

Your firm has been asked to create an informational booklet for the Board of Exchange. This booklet will be printed on yellow paper and will use blue as a spot color.

1. Create a new file. Note: page size is 5.5 inches x 11 inches. This publication will have 10 double-sided, facing pages.

2. Go to the master pages.

3. Create a two-column layout with columns of equal width.

4. Define a style sheet for the footers that will appear at the bottom of the master pages. The style sheet could be named FOOTER and the specifications should be font, Serif (Times); size, 12 point.

5. Define a style sheet for headings. Name the sheet HEADING and the specifications should be font, Sans Serif (Helvetica); size, 24 point; style, italic and bold; left-justified text.

6. Define a style sheet for body copy. Name the sheet BODY COPY and the specifications should be font, Serif (Times); size, 10 point; paragraph indent, .25 inch; space after paragraph, 0.125; widow/orphan protection on; hyphenation off.

7. Below the bottom margin at the left margin of the left master page, create a footer using the footer style sheet that includes the page number marker and the words **The Marketplace.** Behind the page number marker place the graphic SQUARE. Scale the graphic so that it is slightly larger than the page number. The footer **The Marketplace** should not touch the graphic. Refer to plan U4.2.

8. Specify that the graphic is spot color blue.

9. Below the bottom margin at the right margin of the right master page, create a similar footer but the folio should read **Board of Exchange.** Copy the graphic from the left master page to achieve consistency in size.

10. Create pages 2 through 5 according to plans U4.2 and U4.3.

11. Add pages 6 through 9.
12. Create pages 6 through 9 according to plans U4.4 and U4.5.
13. Mark the text in each of the article headings for a table of contents if possible. Create page 1 according to plan U4.1 using the table of contents text or by typing the text in on page 1.
14. Edit the footer style sheet so that the style of the text will be italic. All footers should automatically change to italic throughout the publication.
15. Save the document as UNIT4.
16. Proof your work. Make any changes or corrections. Save again if necessary.
17. Print UNIT4 specifying that you are printing for spot color with crop marks. (Refer to pages 144 through 148 for examples of your output.
18. Proof the printed document. Make corrections and print again if necessary.
19. Close the file.

> Complete the entire exercise before answering the review questions.

Review

1. What is the procedure for adding pages to your document?

2. What is the advantage of creating style sheets?

3. How will specifying spot color change the output of your document?

4. How and why does one use registration marks?

5. Why are master pages important for color publications?

PLAN U4.1

5.5" x 11"   10 pages/double sided   blue

Action in the Marketplace

filename: SQUARE blue squares

What is a Futures Market?

The Auction in Action

A Close Look at the Board of Exchange

Glossary

Board of Exchange 1

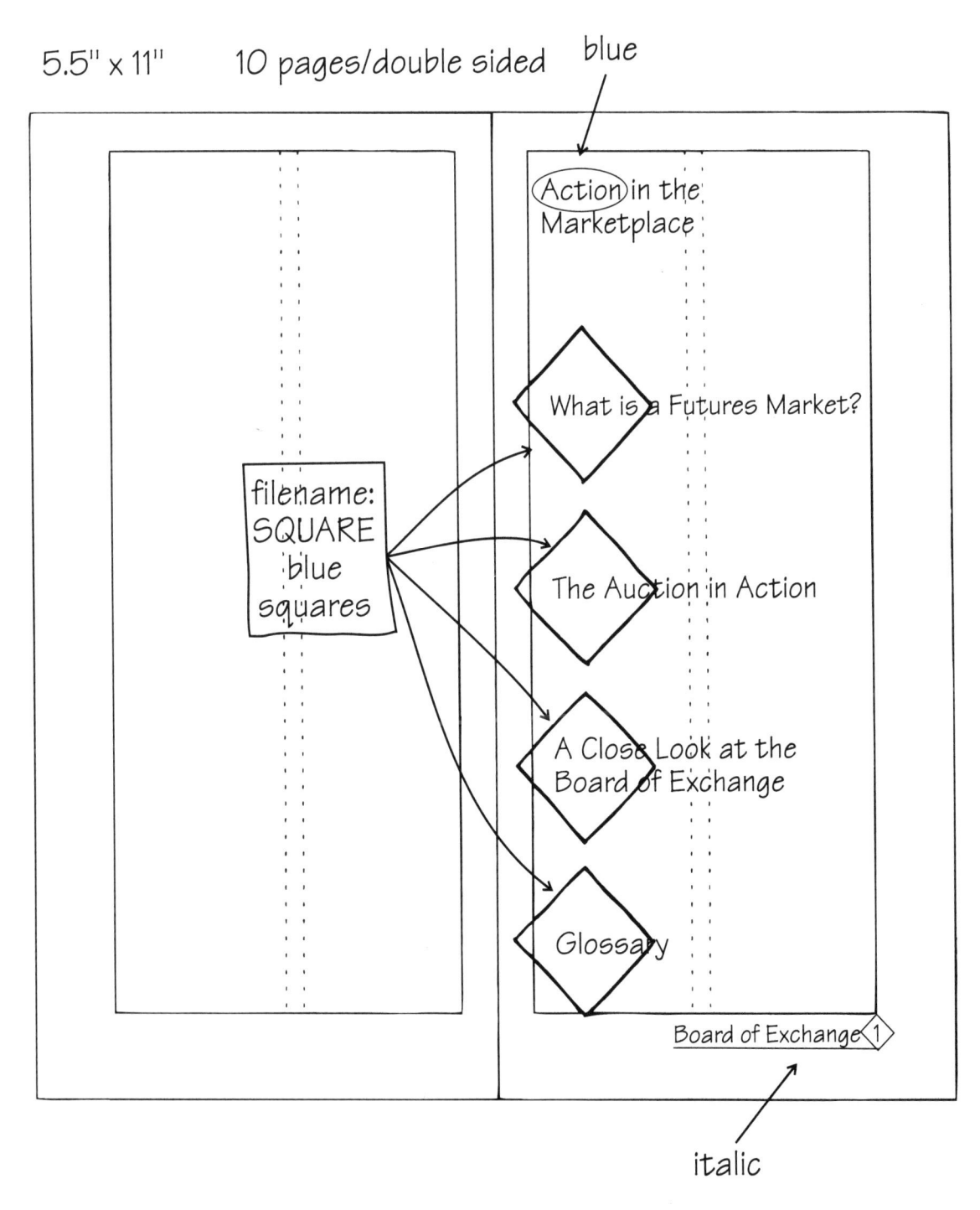

italic

Unit 4 Performance Challenge • 139

PLAN U4.2

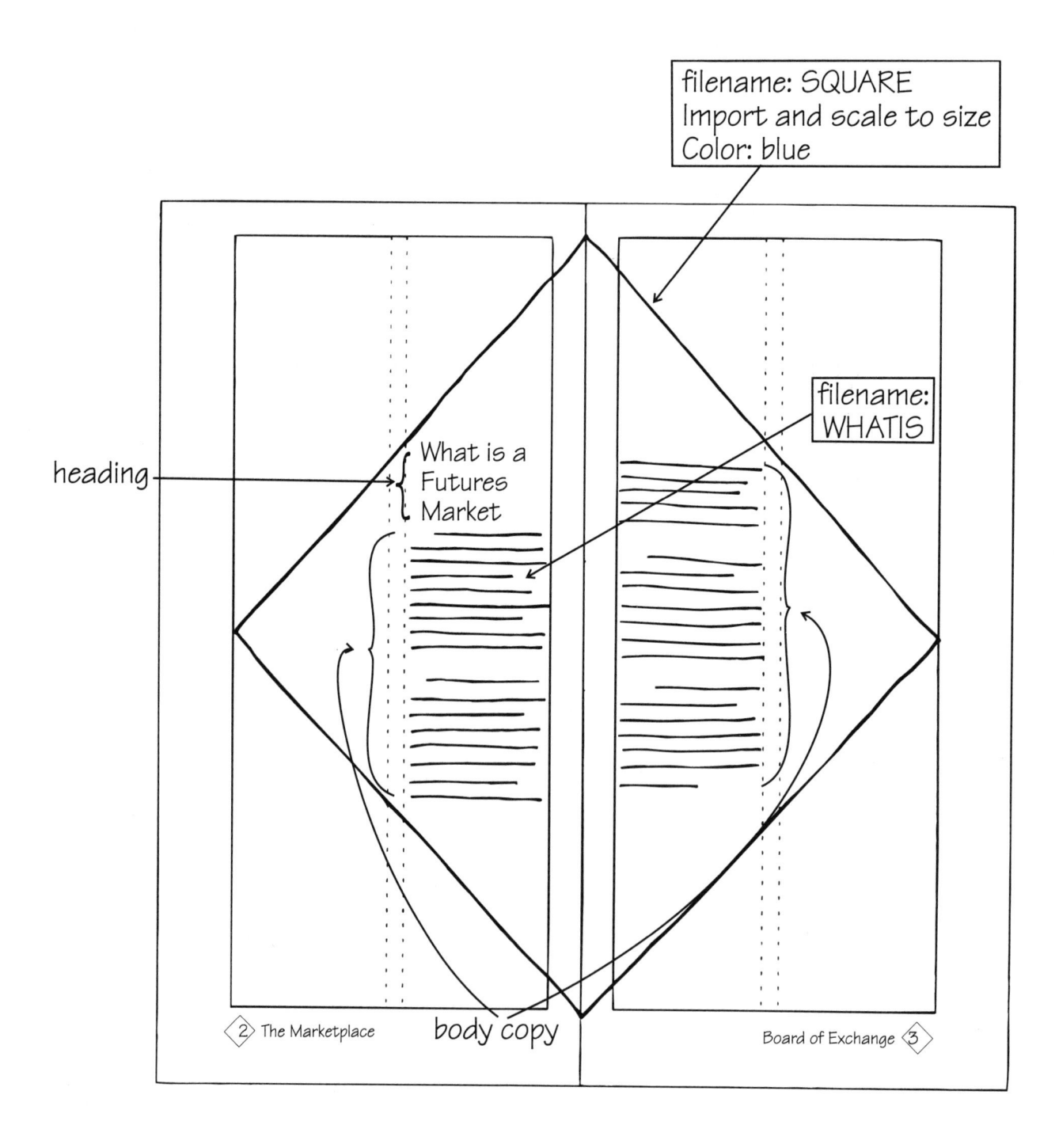

filename: SQUARE
Import and scale to size
Color: blue

filename: WHATIS

heading → What is a Futures Market

body copy

② The Marketplace

Board of Exchange ③

PLAN U4.3

Place graphic so top point touches the top margin between columns 1 and 2 on page 4.

graphic filename: CARDS
Color: black or try spot color blue

The Auction in Action

filename: AUCTION

3"
2"

④ The Marketplace

Board of Exchange ⑤

Place holder for photograph bleeds off right margin, 100% black shade, 3" x 2"

Unit 4 Performance Challenge • 141

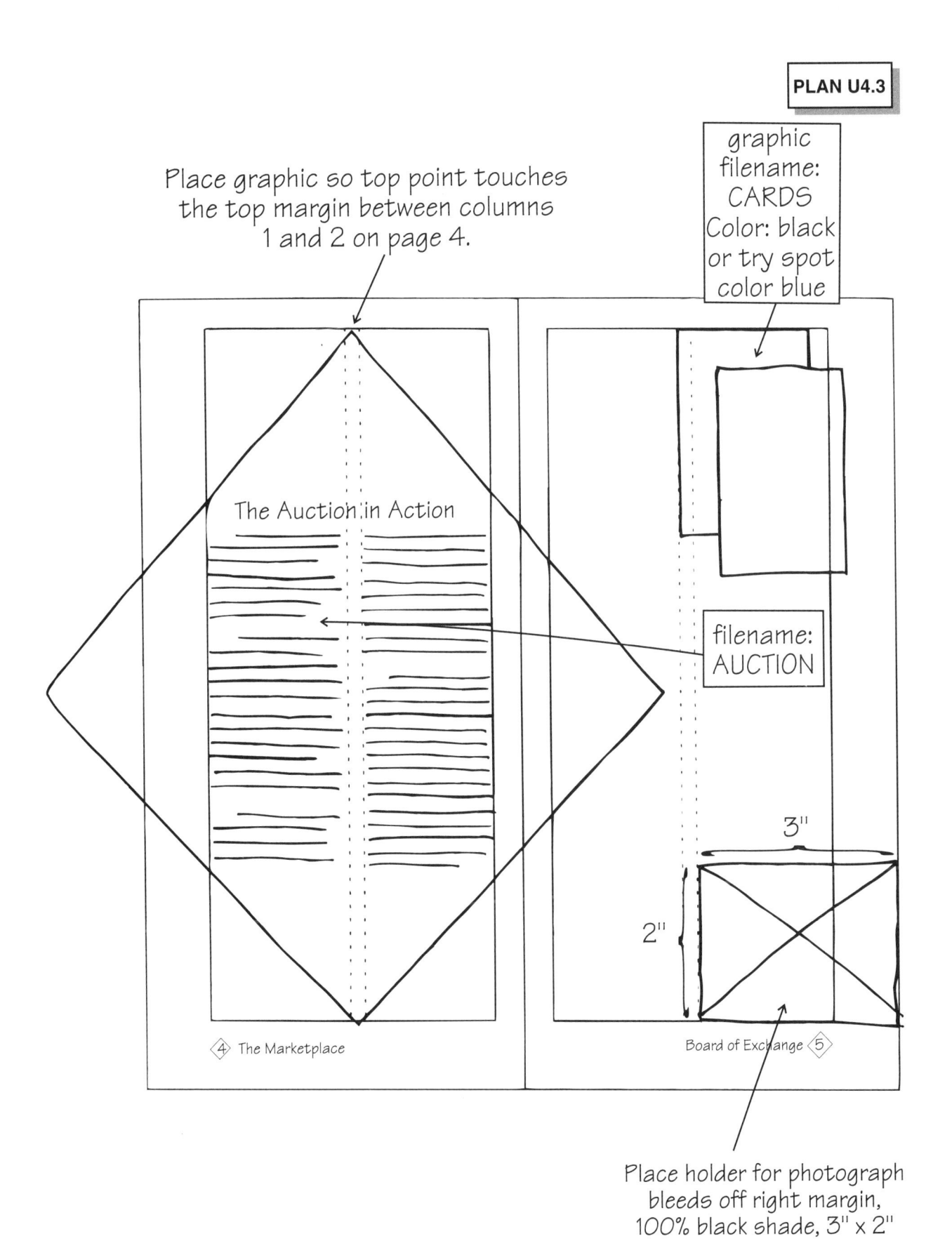

PLAN U4.4

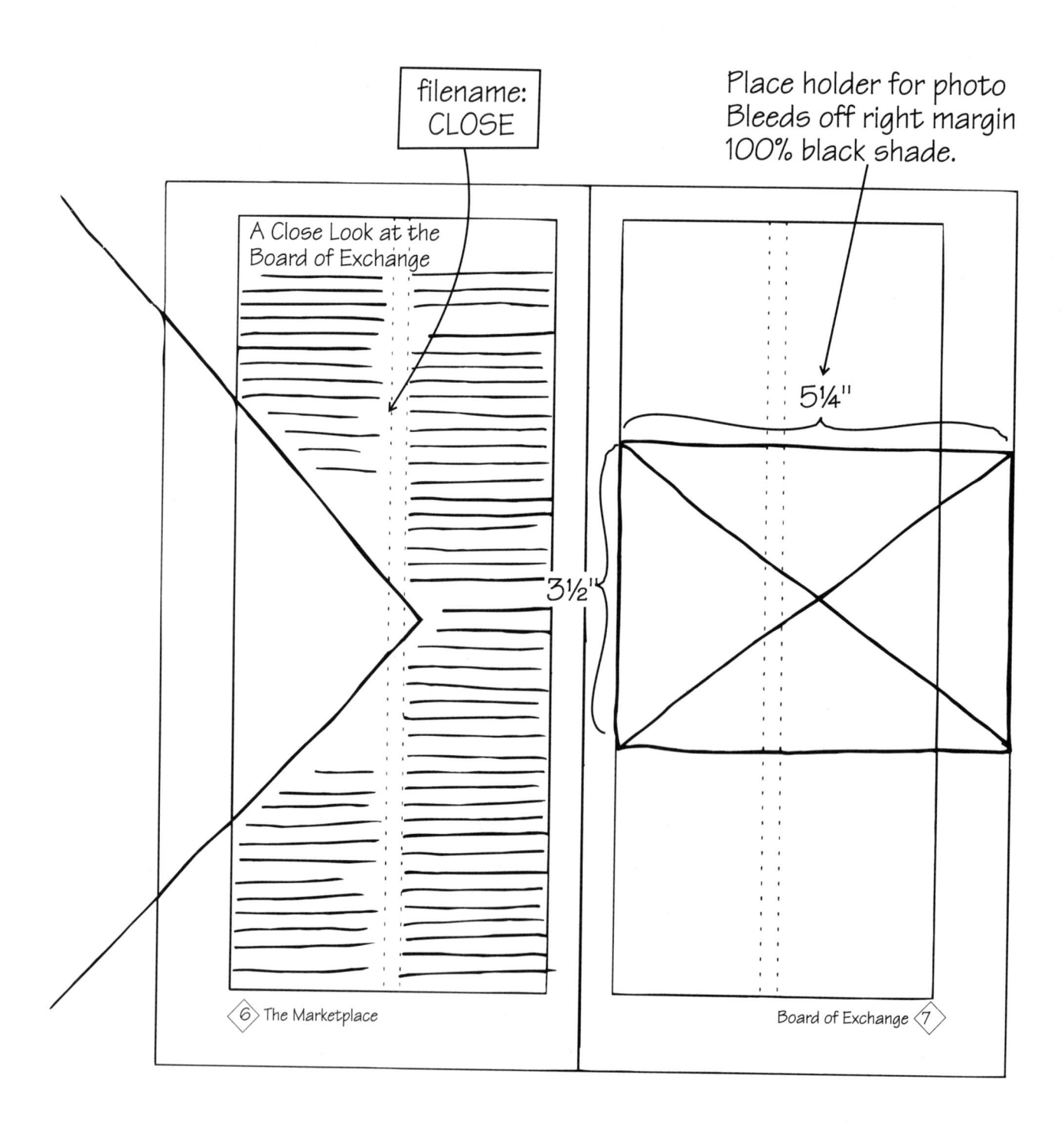

filename: CLOSE

Place holder for photo
Bleeds off right margin
100% black shade.

A Close Look at the Board of Exchange

5¼"

3½"

6 The Marketplace

Board of Exchange 7

PLAN U4.5

graphic filename:
SQUARE
Scale and color blue

Columns arranged in a stair-step fashion.

Glossary

Commodity Futures Trading Commission (CFTC)

bid

hedge

floor broker

option

futures contract

speculator

liquid market

All words to be defined will be printed in blue.

filename: GLOSSARY

5¼"

3½"

⟨8⟩ The Marketplace

Board of Exchange ⟨9⟩

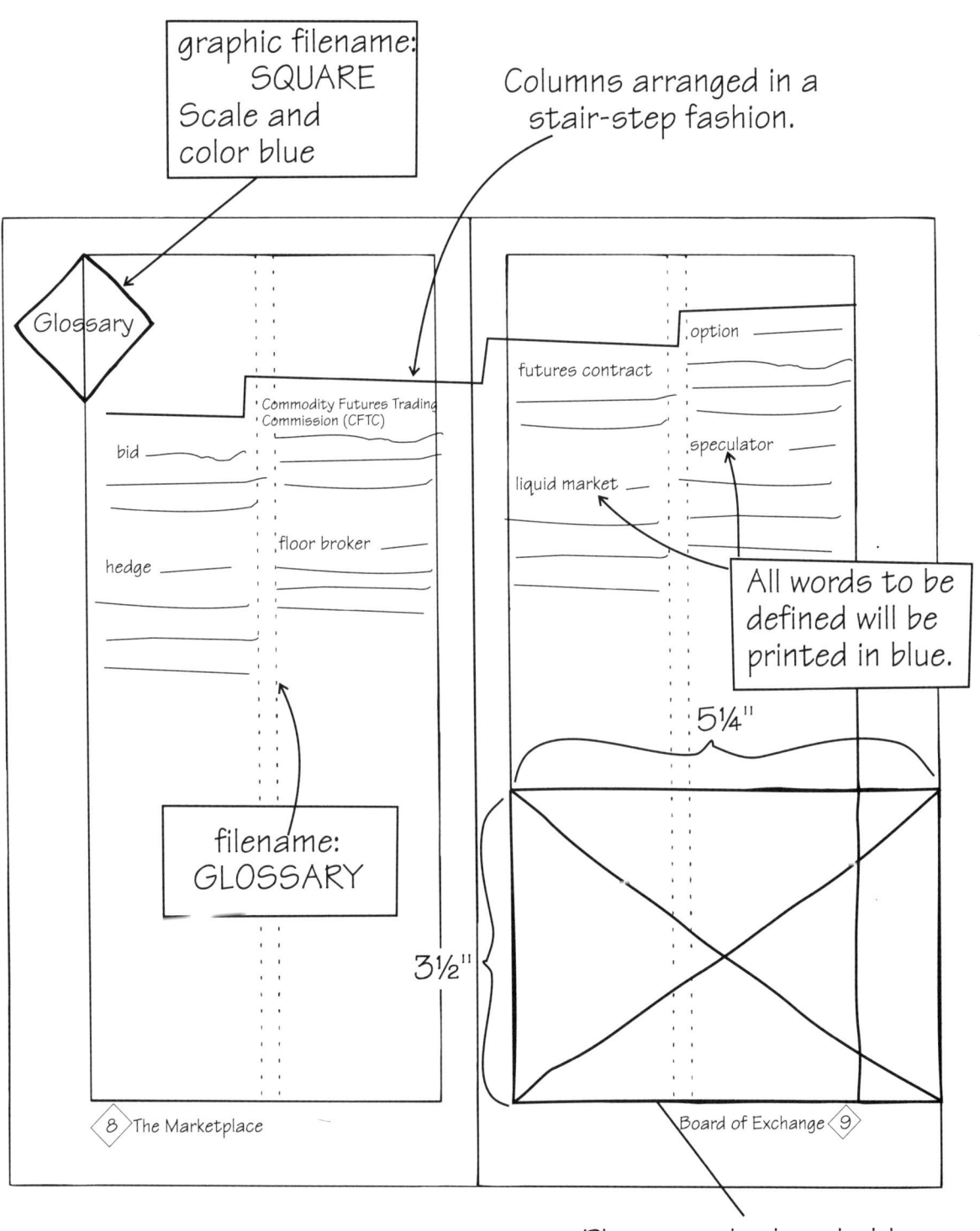

Photograph place holder, 100% black shade.

Unit 4 Performance Challenge • 143

UNIT 4

Black overlay

1

in the Marketplace

What is a Future's Market?

The Auction in Action

A Close Look at the Board of Exchange

Glossary

Board of Exchange 1

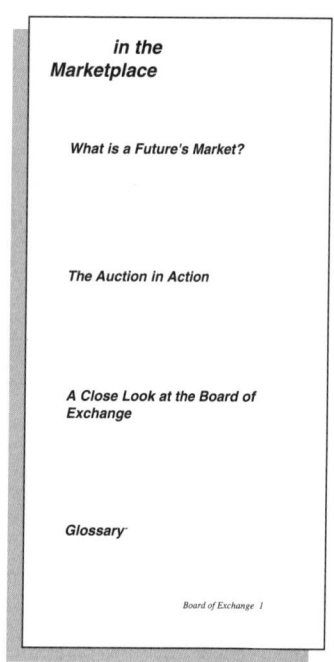

PANTONE 2725 CV overlay

1

Action

144 • Unit 4 Performance Challenge

Black overlay

2   3

What is a Future's Market?

Commodity exchanges such as the Board of Exchange do not determine prices. They are free markets where the forces that influence price are determined in open auction. As the needs and expectations of hedgers and speculators converge on the exchange floor, trades are made and prices areset. Both long-range and short-range factors influence price.

Long-range factors include: price-support programs; credit conditions; changing cost of production, which cause variations in the price of the final product; and population increases, which will increase demand.

Some short-range factors include weather and crop conditions, the carry-over of a particular commodity from the previous crop year, the general level of interest rates, and the international exchange values of currencies. The general level of all commodity prices may influence any single commodity.

Seasonal price factors affect the grain market. Also, because there are periods of gradual rises and periods of slowly sinking prices, it is necessary to be aware of the price trends of all commodities in order to study the trend of one or two.

An observer of basic market situations will find that the forces of nature plus the buying and selling habits of producers and users, often create measurable patterns.

2 *The Marketplace*

Board of Exchange 3

PANTONE 2725 CV overlay

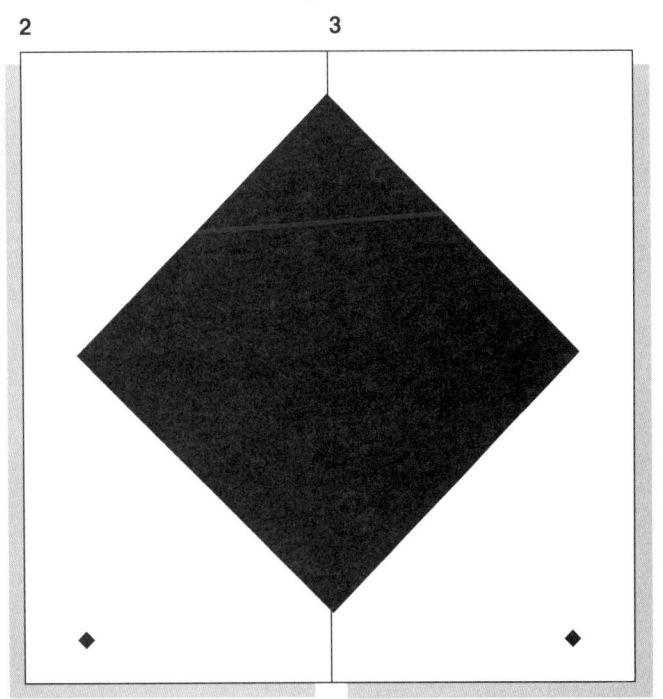

2   3

Unit 4 Performance Challenge • **145**

Black overlay

4　　　　　　　　　　　　　　5

The Auction in Action

Most visitors seeing the trading floor for the first time ask, "What do those hand signals mean?" The Rules and Regulations of the Exchange require pit traders to use open outcry in buying and selling. In addition, they use standard hand signals to clarify their verbal bids and offers, particularly when trading is highly active.

The position of the hands tells whether a trader is buying or selling: a trader has the palm of his hand facing himself if he is buying and his palm facing outward if he is selling. Holding the arm and the fingers of the hand in a horizontal position, a trader shows with finger signals the price at which he is making his bid or offer.

Hand signals also indicate the number of contracts a trader wishes to buy or sell. For grains, each finger held in a vertical position indicates 5,000 bushels or one contract. Offers to buy or sell are made by open outcry so that any trader in the pit who wishes to take the opposite side of the trade may do so.

Each trader lists completed transactions on a trading card or multipart order form. The cards are printed in two colors—one side in blue for "bought" trades and the reverse in red for "sold" trades. Any trade that has been recorded on the card as a grain trade shows the number of bushels involved, the grain, the delivery month of the contract, the price, the number of the clearing firm that is the other principal, the initials of the other broker, and an alphabetic symbol that indicates the half hour in which the trade was executed. These trading cards or order forms constitute the original record and from them the essential data are transferred to the offices of the firms involved.

4　The Marketplace　　　　　　　　　　　　　　Board of Exchange　5

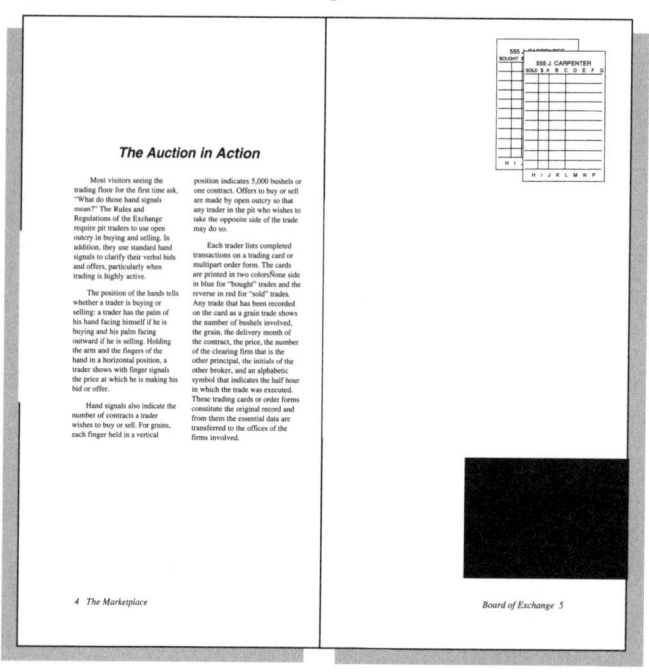

PANTONE 2725 CV overlay

4　　　　　　　　　　　　　　5

146 • Unit 4 Performance Challenge

Black overlay

6   7

A Close Look at the Board of Exchange

The Board of Exchange is a membership association with many of the characteristics of a corporation. It has several types of memberships, with each having access to all or some of the contract markets listed at the Exchange.

Members include independent traders, producers, processors, exporters, brokerage house representatives, banks, and investment bankers. A membership is sold through a bid-and-ask system only when one becomes available for sale. Certain financial requirements have to be met and two Exchange members must sponsor the applicant.

The association is self-governing, with a Board of Directors that includes an elected chairman, vice chairman, 20 member directors, 4 public directors, and the Exchange president. The Exchange is administered by an executive staff headed by an appointed president, one executive vice president, and 4 vice presidents. Currently, more than 50 member committees are responsible for policy-making for all phases of Exchange activity.

Futures orders, most of which originate outside of the Exchange, are received on the trading floor by telephone. To handle the thou- sands of calls coming from commercial traders or from brokerage firms, batteries of telephone stations are strategically located near the pits. Orders received by phone clerks from various member firms are time-stamped, then rushed by messengers (who are called runners) to brokers in the pit for execution. The price at which a trade is made, and other pertinent information, is jotted down by the broker on an order blank that is returned by messenger to his firm's phone desk. The information is then relayed to the office where the order originated so a customer may be advised that the trade is completed. It is not unusual for a customer in another city to be notified of completion of his order less than two minutes after he placed it with his brokerage firm.

6 The Marketplace   *Board of Exchange 7*

PANTONE 2725 CV overlay

6   7

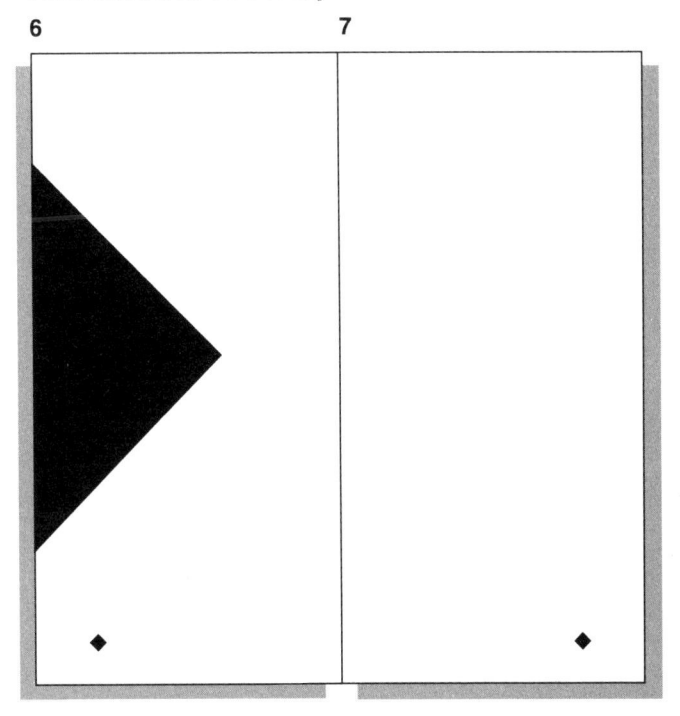

147

Black overlay

8   9

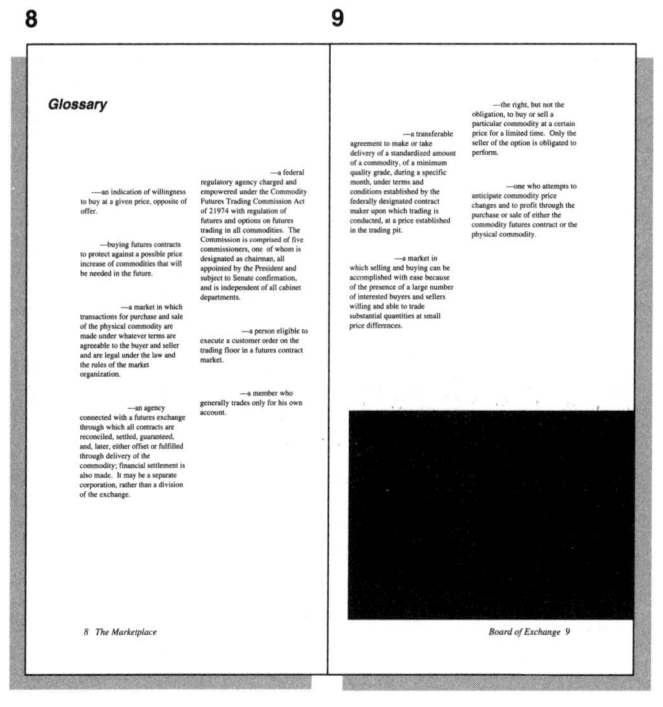

Glossary

—an indication of willingness to buy at a given price, opposite of offer.

—buying futures contracts to protect against a possible price increase of commodities that will be needed in the future.

—a market in which transactions for purchase and sale of the physical commodity are made under whatever terms are agreeable to the buyer and seller and are legal under the law and the rules of the market organization.

—an agency connected with a futures exchange through which all contracts are reconciled, settled, guaranteed, and, later, either offset or fulfilled through delivery of the commodity; financial settlement is also made. It may be a separate corporation, rather than a division of the exchange.

—a federal regulatory agency charged and empowered under the Commodity Futures Trading Commission Act of 21974 with regulation of futures and options on futures trading in all commodities. The Commission is comprised of five commissioners, one of whom is designated as chairman, all appointed by the President and subject to Senate confirmation, and is independent of all cabinet departments.

—a person eligible to execute a customer order on the trading floor in a futures contract market.

—a member who generally trades only for his own account.

—a transferable agreement to make or take delivery of a standardized amount of a commodity, of a minimum quality grade, during a specific month, under terms and conditions established by the federally designated contract maker upon which trading is conducted, at a price established in the trading pit.

—a market in which selling and buying can be accomplished with ease because of the presence of a large number of interested buyers and sellers willing and able to trade substantial quantities at small price differences.

—the right, but not the obligation, to buy or sell a particular commodity at a certain price for a limited time. Only the seller of the option is obligated to perform.

—one who attempts to anticipate commodity price changes and to profit through the purchase or sale of either the commodity futures contract or the physical commodity.

8 The Marketplace   *Board of Exchange 9*

PANTONE 2725 CV overlay

8   9

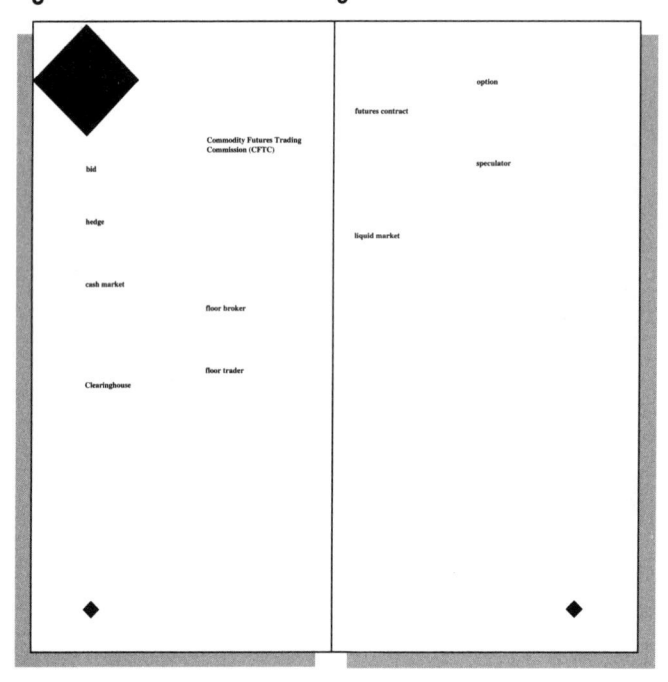

bid

hedge

cash market

Clearinghouse

Commodity Futures Trading Commission (CFTC)

floor broker

floor trader

option

futures contract

speculator

liquid market

148

Glossary

Glossary

A

Automatic hyphenation A function that directs software to hyphenate text automatically.

B

Balance In graphic design, the placement of elements on a page so that each complements or physically balances the other. White space is considered a design element.

Bi-fold Publication printed on a single page folded in half.

Body copy The main text or portion of a document; also called body text.

Bold A type style that is a heavy, darker version of a typeface.

Bleed Graphic elements that are printed to the edge of the page leaving no margins or white space.

Byline Author's name that appears after the title of an article.

C

Center align To line up text in the middle of a page or column.

Close To quit working on a current publication.

Column guides The vertical, nonprinting lines that mark the left and right edges of columns.

Column width The horizontal measure of the column.

Copyfitting Procedure for estimating space requirements for text and illustrations.

Crop To trim the unwanted portions of a graphic.

D

Default A setting or value automatically used by a system unless you specify otherwise.

Design The specifications covering use of type, illustrations, and other elements in a publication.

Desktop publishing An electronic method of combining text and graphics to produce professional quality documents.

Double-sided publication A publication that will be reproduced on both sides of a sheet of paper.

Drop shadow A shaded repetition of a shape positioned slightly to the left or right of the original shape.

Dummy A layout that designates placement of elements in a publication.

E

Edit To change text, graphics, or specifications in a publication.

Element A unit of type or an illustration to be included in a publication.

Enlarged initial letter The first letter in the first word of a paragraph is set larger than the other letters.

F

Facing pages In a double-sided publication, the two pages that face each other when the publication is open. The even-number page will be on the left and the odd-number pages will be on the right. The layout of facing pages is designed as a unit.

Folio a line of type on the page that gives information about the chapter, section, topic, page number, etc.

Font The complete assortment of characters for one typeface at one size. It includes uppercase and lowercase characters, figures, and punctuation marks.

Footer One or more lines of text that appear at the bottom of every page.

G

Graphic Line art or halftone (photograph) to be included in a layout.

Guide A nonprinting dotted or dashed line that can be created to help with alignment of text or graphics.

Gutter The space at the inside margins of two facing pages or the blank space between columns.

H

Halftone Dot pattern used to reproduce photos and other continuous-tone illustrations.

Header One or more lines of text that appear at the top of every page.

Headline Unit of type that titles a story or article.

I

Import Bring a saved file into a publication.

Insert To add additional text in an existing text block.

Italic Typeface with characters that slant to the right.

J

Justify To align text so that it lines up evenly at both the left and the right margin.

K

Kern To adjust the spacing between letters.

L

Landscape A page orientation that has a greater width than height.

Layout Arrangement of text and graphics on a page.

Leading (pronounced "ledding") The amount of vertical spacing, expressed in points, between the tops of the capital letters in two successive lines of text.

Legends Graphic representation of what appears on a diagram, map, or graph.

Logo A design element that represents a company or an institution.

M

Margins The top, bottom, left, and right edges of a page that are outside the body text or graphic image.

Master page A page or separate menu in which the user can store the layout elements that repeat in all the pages in a publication.

Masthead Section of a publication giving its title, details of publication, etc.

N

Newsletter A periodical that delivers information to a specialized audience.

O

Orphan A word or single short line of text ending a paragraph at the top of a column.

Overhead transparency An acetate sheet for use on an overhead projector.

P

Pica Unit of measure equal to one-sixth of an inch. Twelve points equal one pica.

Point size Standard unit of measure for type. A point equals 1/12 pica or 1/72 inch.

Portrait A page orientation that has a greater height than width.

Poster A large sign that conveys a message.

Presentation graphic A publication used in a lecture, such as a slide or overhead transparency of a chart or graph.

Price list A document that gives pricing, packing, shipping, and other information needed to order products.

Product information sheet A document, usually a single page, that describes an individual product, a single family of products, or a service.

Proofreading Quality control procedure for correcting errors.

Proportional characters Characters designed so that some characters, such as "w," take up more horizontal space than others such as "l."

R

Ragged right Description of type column with an unjustified right margin.

Readability The ease of reading a page. Factors affecting readability include type size and spacing.

Resize To change the dimensions of a graphic.

Reverse lines White rules on contrasting black, shaded, or colored background.

Right justified The even alignment of text along the right margin.

Rotation A feature that moves text or a graphic as specified by the user.

Rule A horizontal or vertical line often used to enhance the design or readability of a publication.

Ruler guides Horizontal and vertical dotted lines that are nonprinting extensions of the rulers and are used for aligning text and graphics on a page.

S

Sans serif A style of type with no serifs.

Scaling The increasing or decreasing of a graphic.

Serif Horizontal lines added to type characters for design and readability.

Shade A degree of tint used to fill an area.

Soft hyphen A hyphen placed temporarily at the end of a line to support automatic spacing and justification of text. The soft hyphen is eliminated if the text is altered.

Standoff The distance between the outside edge of a graphic element and the closest copy element.

Style sheet A set of type specifications entered through a dialog box and used to format type.

Subheading A title or heading introducing a subtopic in the main body text.

T

Text block Text element on a page layout, usually refers to columns of type.

Tile In an oversize publication, that portion of the page that is printed on a single sheet of paper. To make a complete page, you must assemble and paste together the tiles.

Tabloid A page size setting, usually 11 by 17 inches.

Template A dummy publication that acts as a model or starting point, providing the structure and general layout for another similar publication.

Typeface An assortment of characters of one particular kind of type.

Type size The height of a typeface measured in points.

Type style An assortment of styles of a typeface, such as italic and bold.

W

White space The blank space on a page. In page design, the white space must be balanced with the printed parts of the page.

Widow A single word at the bottom of a paragraph or a single word or short line at the top of a page.

WYSIWYG (what you see is what you get) A video display in the same format as the printed text to be developed.